BASKET
ESSENTIALS
RIB BASKET WEAVING

BASKET ESSENTIALS
RIB BASKET WEAVING

Techniques and Projects for DIY Woven Reed Baskets

Lora S. Irish

FOX CHAPEL
PUBLISHING

Basket Essentials: Rib Basket Weaving is an original work, first published in 2020 by Fox Chapel Publishing Company, Inc. All rights reserved. No part of this publication may be reproduced, stored in a retrieval system or transmitted, in any form or by any means, electronic, mechanical, photocopying, recording or otherwise, without the prior written permission of the copyright holders.

ISBN 978-1-4971-0014-5

Library of Congress Control Number:2020930321

To learn more about the other great books from Fox Chapel Publishing,
or to find a retailer near you, call toll-free 800-457-9112
or visit us at *www.FoxChapelPublishing.com*.

We are always looking for talented authors. To submit an idea,
please send a brief inquiry to acquisitions@foxchapelpublishing.com.

Printed in Singapore
First printing

Dedication

For Ayleen, Gretchen, Paul, Katie, and especially Colleen—
my manuscript editors—who over the years have teased,
pulled, dragged, harangued, weaseled, yanked, squeezed,
extracted, wrestled, and even guilted me into getting that one
more answer, one more definition, one more measurement,
or one more step. The very things that make Fox Chapel
books such a delight! I thank each one of you!

Acknowledgments

I wish to extend my deepest thanks to Tiffany Hill, Colleen
Dorsey, and Wendy Reynolds for their excellent work in the
creation, development, and refinement of this manuscript.
As an author, it is a wonderful experience to be working with
such a well-skilled team.

Contents

75

83

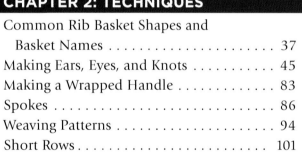

23

100

108

130

185

188

CHAPTER 3: STEP-BY-STEP BASKETS

CHAPTER 4: ADDITIONAL BASKETS

What Is a Rib Basket?

Basket names can seem so confusing. Creel, angling, and shopping baskets are named for their uses and main purposes. Egg baskets, stair baskets, and hearth baskets refer to their specific shapes. Rattan, wicker, and reed baskets are named for the materials with which they are woven. And coiled, twined, woven, and plaited baskets refer to the weaving techniques used to create them.

Rib baskets, named for the technique that makes the main basket structure or framework, are created using a rim hoop that can be either one joined piece of wood or something made from entwined branches and vines that creates the circular opening structure of the basket. Many rib baskets also use a hoop that is centered at a 90-degree angle to the rim hoop and that is used as the spine of and handle for the basket.

From the two center points of the rim hoop or the intersection of the rim hoop and handle hoop, new spokes are added to the basket sides in a half-wheel spoke arrangement. An ear pattern is woven to lock the hoops to the spokes, working from the rim hoop down and out. Once the hoops and spokes are locked, you can use a variety of weaving patterns and weaving materials to fill in the sides of your basket. As the basket grows, you can add more spokes, further defining the basket's final shape.

Throughout this comprehensive guide to rib baskets, you'll learn everything you need to know; we will explore the rim hoops that you can use, how to add handle hoops, how to weave your locking ear patterns, how to add and anchor your spokes, how the length of the spokes defines the final shape of the basket, and more.

As you work your first baskets, remember that basketry is a very organic art form that uses natural materials that vary in thickness, width, and moisture content. Even with the most careful measurements, precise cutting, and expert weaving skills, no two baskets are ever identical. So, relax, have fun, and let's learn the art behind rib baskets together.

CHAPTER 1

GETTING STARTED

A Note on the Imprecision of Basket Making

The art of basketry—whether rib, woven reed, or willow—is not an exacting craft. It is a back-porch, natural-materials, intuitive art form that has been passed down from one generation to the next. Basket shapes, sizes, uses, materials, terminology, and weaving patterns can change dramatically from one region of the world to the next. Seldom does even the most experienced basket maker create two identically sized designs, and often you will discover that your basket can be classified under several different names or categories of shape (more on this on page 37).

Unlike knitting, where a rigid set of stitches must be made to create a specific pattern, or woodworking, where exact measurements must be made to ensure a tight, accurate fit between pieces, in basketry, basket makers must be ready to adjust and alter their work with each new step to compensate for changes in how deeply a spoke can be inserted, the tension of a weave, the natural weaving abilities of a material, the dampness of the weaving material, and the weaving pattern being used.

As an example, you will discover that the reed size charts on page 24 give approximate sizes only. Reed is a key material in basket making, but the actual size or measurement of a reed can vary because of several factors:

- Was the reed originally cut to imperial (US) or metric measurements? What might have been cut to a ⅜" width using imperial measurements will measure 9.525mm in metric. If it was cut using metric measurements, it may have originally measured 9.5mm, which would be equivalent to 0.374016 inches—not a natural number to someone using the US system. Because these conversion measurements are far too exacting to be of any real use to the basket maker, you will discover that a ⅜" reed will be noted as approximately 9.5mm—rounded up or down to the nearest size.

- Was the reed originally cut by the manufacturer slightly damp or bone dry? If the reed was cut damp to a 2mm size, it may only measure 1.75mm after it loses its natural moisture content, yet it may measure 2.25mm after it has been soaked in water in preparation for use.

- Has the reed been stored in an open-air environment where it can absorb humidity, or has it been stored in a closed, dry bag? Reed absorbs the moisture from the air and will swell to a slightly larger size if stored in open air than it would if stored dry.

As you can see, reed sizes are a great example of how imprecision is a natural part of basket making. But they are just one example of many!

Here's another: While I will provide measurements for your spokes throughout the projects and lessons in this book, these measurements reflect my finished,

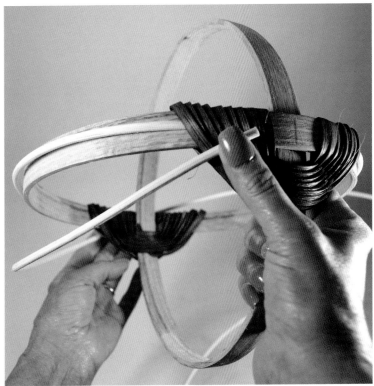

Cut spokes to size after holding them up against your basket.

adjusted sizes that fit my basket using my particular round reed size. To create that finished basket size, I cut my spokes slightly (about ⅜" to ½" [1 to 1.3cm]) longer than what I expected to need. Then I cut them to a tapered point so they could be inserted into the ear or previous weaving patterns. In the photo on page 11, you can see me eyeballing a spoke and getting ready to cut it to size.

After the new spoke has been inserted, I visually check its placement against the curved profile of the spokes that have already been added to the basket frame. In the photo at top right, you can see that the spoke that I am holding is placed too deeply into the previous weaving work to conform with the desired profile curve of the basket frame.

By adjusting the placement of that spoke, pulling it out slightly from the weaving pattern, I can bring it out to the curve of the desired profile, as shown in the photo at bottom right. You may need to adjust a spoke several times during the weaving process.

All of this imprecision, estimation, and adjustment on the fly are actually a great advantage to this craft: you, the basket maker, need not worry about extremely accurate measurements, substituting one reed size for another, or how many rows it takes to fill one area of your basket. If you use a fatter round reed spoke than the one I use, or if your spoke needs to be ½" (1.3cm) longer than mine, your basket will still be a delightful, unique, and functional masterpiece!

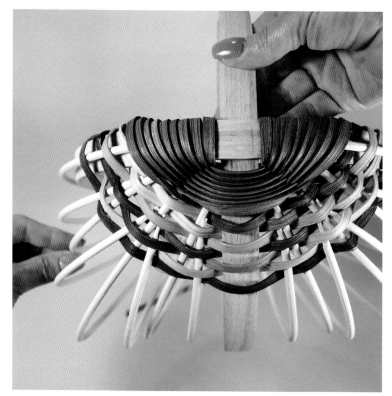

Check spoke placement after the spokes are inserted.

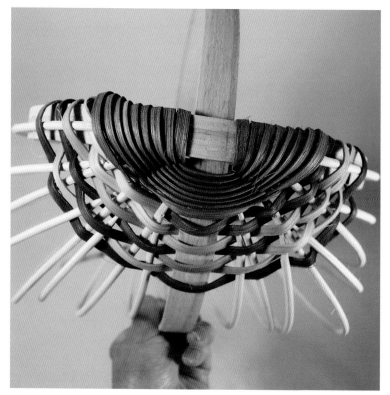

Once the shape looks right, keep weaving!

Essential Basket-Making Terms

Every craft has its own special vocabulary. Because basketry is a folk art handed down from one generation to the next, each region seems to have its own terms for the structural framework of its baskets, basket shapes, and weaving patterns. For example, the weaving pattern that locks the handle hoop to the rim hoop can be called an ear, an eye, or a knot.

Let's take a quick look at the basic terms used in rib basket construction and how you can apply them in working your own unique designs. Many of these terms are used in other kinds of basket making as well, although some are specific to the rib baskets this book focuses on. Make sure you take a good look at this list of terms before diving further into the book, to avoid confusion later! The terms are presented in a logical order rather than in alphabetical order both to help you understand them and to serve as an introduction to how rib baskets are constructed.

hoop: a continuous circle, oval, or other shape made of wood (or sometimes another material) that is used to form the handle, the rim, and often the spine of a rib basket.

handle: the upper portion of the center vertical hoop.

rim handle: an open, unwoven area along the rim hoop that creates a space for a full hand grip.

handle/handle hoop

God's Eye knot

half God's Eye knot

rim/rim hoop

spine/central spoke

spokes/ribs

weavers

rim/rim hoop: the hoop that sits horizontally and acts as the rim/opening of the basket. The spokes are attached to the rim with weaving.

spoke/rib: a foundational piece of a rib basket that is typically attached at both ends to the rim at the site of the ear/knot anchoring the handle and rim together. Multiple spokes/ribs plus the rim and handle form the essential "skeleton" of the basket, before weavers are added. Throughout this book, we'll use the term "spoke" rather than "rib" to refer to additional pieces that are inserted into the ear/eye (but both terms are accurate!).

spine/central spoke: the spoke or bottom portion of the handle hoop that is placed at a 90-degree angle to the rim, going from one side of the rim all the way to the very bottom of the basket and back up to the opposite side of the rim. Often the handle and spine are made of a single hoop, but the spine can also be made from a separate single spoke in a basket that doesn't have a standard handle.

weaver: any piece, such as a reed, raffia, or a wood splint, that is woven horizontally around the basket spokes or other parts of the basket. Weavers are what are most obviously visible when you look at a basket, whereas spokes tend to be somewhat hidden.

weaving: adding weavers to the skeleton of a basket in any of a variety of patterns by feeding the weavers over and under the spokes of the basket.

reed: a weaving and basketry material that is made from rattan, a large group of species of thorny, vine-like palms. It is cut in long strips from the stems of the plant and dried.

row: a single weaver (or set of weavers as a unit) woven from rim to rim or from the starting and ending point of short rows.

short row: a row of weaving that does not go from rim to rim all the way around the basket one time, instead only incorporating some of the basket spokes. Short rows are used to compensate for the changing circumference of a basket as the spokes increase or decrease in size.

packing: pushing weavers together to make them lie tightly against the previous rows of weavers.

splicing: adding a new weaver to an existing weaver that is too short to finish the desired row.

ear/eye/knot: the lashing that securely connects the rim hoop to the handle hoop or the rim hoop to the spine of the basket frame. There are a variety of ear, eye, and knot weaving patterns that can be interchanged to create new basket designs.

half God's Eye knot: a common knot used to bind the handle to the rim (forming an ear) or used in combination with a smaller eye/ear pattern to create the weaving that will anchor the spokes. It looks like a half circle or fan, facing down on the body of the basket where the handle meets the rim.

God's Eye knot: another common knot used to bind the handle to the rim (forming an ear). It looks like a full circle on the body and handle of the basket where the handle meets the rim. A large God's Eye knot creates the weaving that will anchor the spokes.

Tools

EVERYDAY TOOLS

The basket maker's tool kit requires a few basic tools, many of which you may already have in your general crafting-supplies stash. Some of the essential tools used for basketwork that you may already have lying around include: a bench knife or pair of heavy-bladed scissors, a packing tool or standard-tipped screwdriver, spring clamps or laundry clothespins, an awl, a yardstick or measuring tape, twine or heavy thread, and a large pan for soaking reeds.

CUTTING AND PACKING TOOLS

A tool to cut reeds, a packer, and simple clamps to hold the weavers in place are essential to basket making. Spring clips or spring clamps are also used to anchor spokes to the ear until enough weaving has been worked to hold them securely.

Reed cutters (specially marketed to basket makers), scissors, and utility knives are excellent for cutting flat weaving reeds and round spokes to size. Pick a heavy-bladed pair of scissors that can handle

You may already have some of the everyday items needed for basket making.

the thickest round reeds. A utility knife or bench knife can be used both to cut reeds to length and to taper both ends of a reed to reduce the thickness at an overlap point in the weaving.

Packing tools, or packers, are used to firmly set one row of weaving against another. Packers come with both straight shanks to pack the basket walls

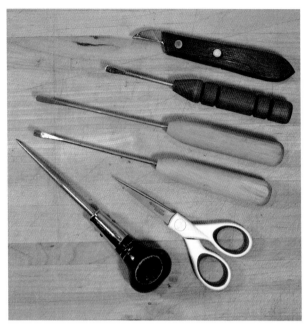

Top to bottom: bench knife, flat-tipped packing tool, long flat-tipped packing tool, curved-tipped packing tool, scissors, large awl.

and bent shanks that will reach into the tight corners of a God's Eye knot or under the rim of a basket. You can use a straight standard screwdriver as a packing tool, too.

An awl is a necessary tool for rib basket makers. This tool has a long, tapered shank that ends in a sharp point. The point is used to split the reeds in a half God's Eye knot to receive a basket spoke.

Spring clamps and spring clothespins (not peg clothespins) are used to temporarily secure a weaver as you work through a weaving pattern. To secure an extra-large round spoke or a natural thick vine, you can use small zip ties or cable ties. Cut the ties after the weaving has been completed enough to hold the spoke or vine in place securely without the help of the ties.

Ceramic clay tools are inexpensive and come in a variety of shapes that you can use in basketry. Most sets include a needlepoint tool that can be used as an awl, flat and arrowhead-shaped tools that can be used as packers, and several types of curved or bent tools that will reach into those hard-to-reach spaces.

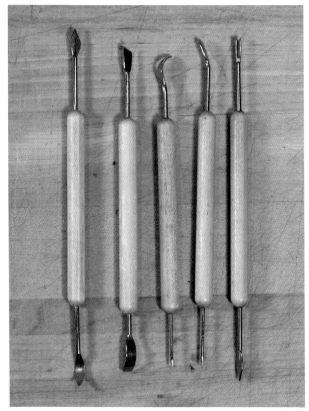

This small set of ceramic clay tools can easily become basket-making tools.

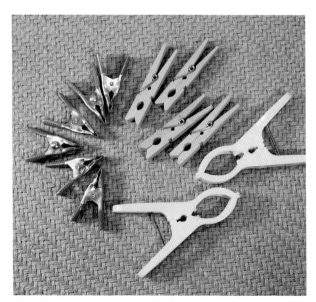

Small spring clamps can hold the previous row of weavers in place as you work a new weaver.

REED SHAVER

A reed shaver has a heavily textured grater on the bottom side of the tool. As you pull the grater along the end of a cut flat weaver, the tool shaves the weaver to a thin taper. Use a reed shaver to taper the two ends of your reed where one end will overlap another.

WEAVING TOOLS

To tease a weaver through an extra-tight area, use either nylon-grip flat-nosed pliers or straight-nosed pliers. The tips of the pliers can grip the reed end when your fingertips are too large. Nylon-grip pliers cushion the damp reed from being damaged by the pliers' tip.

A jeweler's bead scoop has the perfect shape for creating the pathway for added spokes in a rib basket. The

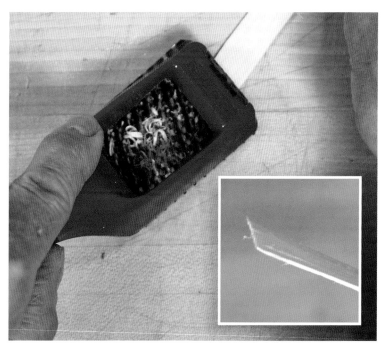

A reed shaver cuts the wood fibers at the end of a reed to reduce the thickness of the reed into a gentle taper. The tapered end makes the reed easier to work with.

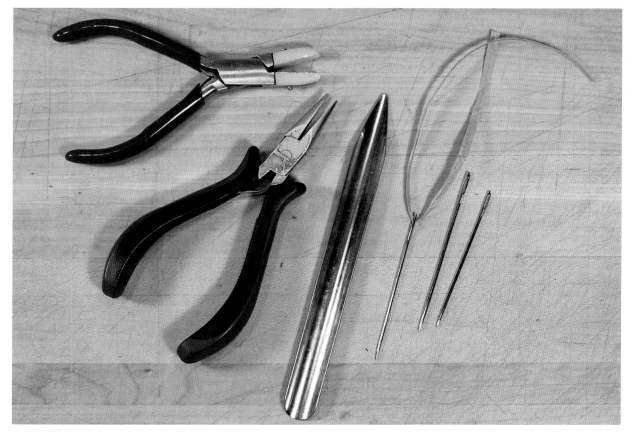

From left to right: nylon-grip flat-nosed pliers, straight-nosed pliers, jeweler's bead scoop, tapestry needles.

point of the scoop is worked into the weaving space where you want to add a new spoke. The new spoke can be guided along the scoop and placed into position.

Tapestry needles or blunt needles for leathercrafting work well to lace raffia, small twine, and ribbon accents along your weaving patterns.

SOAKING TOOLS

Your reeds, whether round or flat, need to be soaked for a few moments in warm water to make them flexible enough to weave smoothly through the ups and downs of a weaving pattern. Soak your reeds in a large water bowl or pan before you begin working. Use a large sea sponge or synthetic sponge and large paintbrushes to redampen your reeds and spokes as you work the basket. Soaking is needed when the reed will be worked over and under spokes that are spaced as close as ¼" (0.6cm) apart. Only soak your reeds right before you will be weaving them into the basket frame. Repeated soaking and drying can make your reed brittle and cause it to lift fine fibers along its surface.

Water bowls, sponges, and paintbrushes serve to soak your reeds and keep them damp during work.

MEASURING TOOLS

You will need a tape measure, yardstick, or cutting mat to measure your round and flat reeds. A tape measure works very well for marking the length of a basket spoke. Reeds being used as weavers, which do not need to be as accurate in length as spokes, can simply be measured against the area of the basket into which they will be woven—just remember to overestimate a little to account for the ins and outs of the weaving.

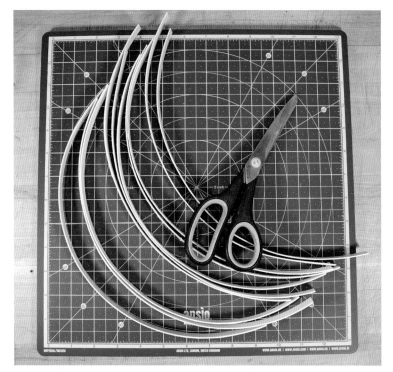

This self-healing quilting mat has both a 1" (2.5cm) grid pattern, which can be used to measure the spokes, and a set of concentric circles, which can be used to check the roundness of the basket spoke pattern.

Weaving Materials

There is a lot of variety in the materials you will use to make your baskets! In the photo below, you can see a preview of just some of that variety. Each of these names, numbers, and descriptions will be explained in detail in the following pages. As you read, refer back to this image to see how they all compare.

HOOPS

Wooden hoops are what give the rib basket its classic round or oval shape. These hoops are used for the handle of the basket (when it has one) as well as the top rim. Hoops typically measure from ½" to 1¼" (1.3 to 3.2cm) in width and from 3" to 18" (7.6 to 45cm) in diameter. The diameter of your hoop determines the general diameter of your basket, because the hoop acts as the basket's opening.

Most basketry hoops are made from oak, but you can also use the inner ring of an embroidery hoop, which can be made of laminated wood layers. Hoops are available in round, oval, rounded square, and rounded rectangle shapes, any of which can be used for either the handle or rim of your rib basket.

Many of the smaller basket designs throughout this book were worked using a 5" to 8" (12 to 20cm) embroidery hoop. While not as sturdy as wider oak

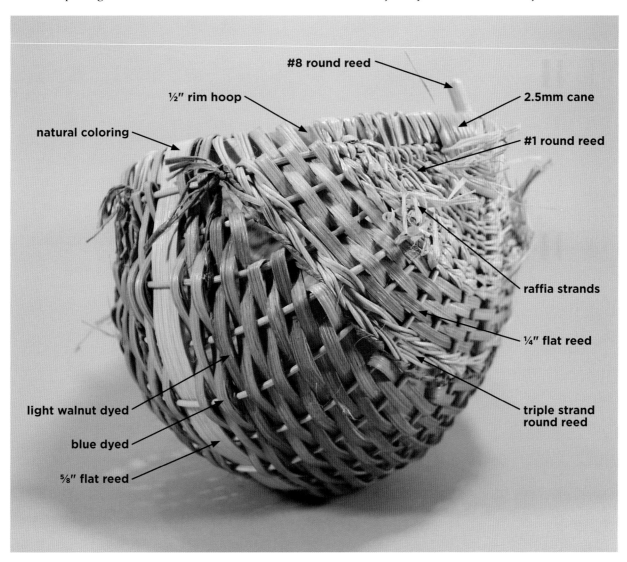

#8 round reed

½" rim hoop

natural coloring

2.5mm cane

#1 round reed

raffia strands

¼" flat reed

triple strand round reed

light walnut dyed

blue dyed

⅝" flat reed

Sanding Hoops

A light sanding, using 220-grit sandpaper, cleans any loose fibers from your basket hoops. It also rounds over the hard, sharp edges along the top and bottom of the hoop that can, over time, cause your weavers to weaken and break.

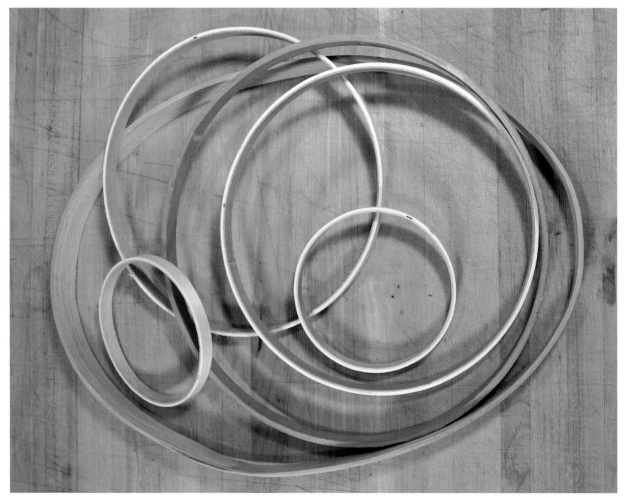

Hoop sizes and shapes vary, and the hoop size and shape will partially determine the overall size and shape of your finished basket.

hoops designed for basketry, these smaller hoops are very economical for the beginner basket maker.

Grapevine, honeysuckle, and wisteria vines can make wonderful natural hoops for your basketwork. Harvest healthy, mature material from your garden. While the vine is freshly cut, wrap it around the bottom of a small planter or bucket that has the diameter and shape that you want for your basket hoop. As you wrap, weave the end of the vine through the wraps that you have already created to interlock the coils. Use twine to tie the coils together in several areas. Let the vine dry on the bucket or planter for several weeks. You can then remove your natural hoop and finish the drying process by hanging the hoop indoors in a dark, dry area. Hoops made from a late summer or early fall harvest will be ready to use in the early spring of the following year.

Try using natural hoops, like grapevine, in your basketwork.

Round Reed Hoops

You can make your own hoops for baskets out of round reeds, a bit like you can use natural materials as hoops.

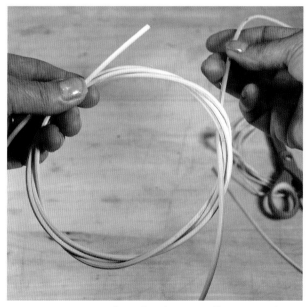

1 Using #3 round reed or larger, roll your reed into a circular coil. Thread the end of the reed through each coil to entwine each new coil as you go.

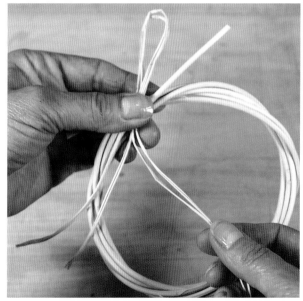

2 About 5" (12.7cm) from one end of a long strand of raffia, fold a loop. Hold the loop and loop tail over the end of the coiled reed.

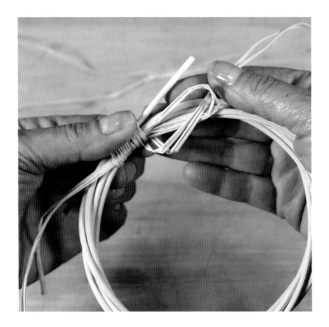

3 Starting 2" (5cm) from the loop fold, wrap the long end of the raffia around your reed coil, covering the loop and the loop tail from step 2. Work the wrap for at least 1" to 1½" (2.5 to 3.8cm). At this point, about 1" (2.5cm) of the loop remains unwrapped. Slide the long wrapping end of the raffia strand through the loop.

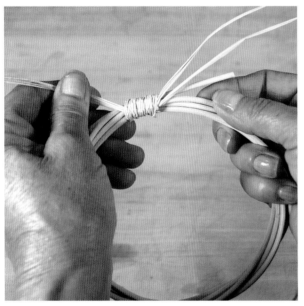

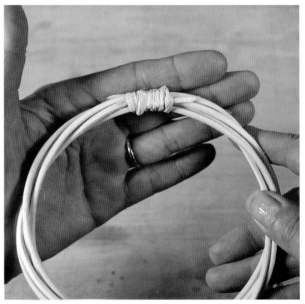

4 Holding both the wrapping end of the raffia and the loop tail, gently pull on the loop tail. This will pull the excess loop followed by the wrapping strand under the wrap. Pull until you have completely hidden the loop under the wrap.

5 Cut any excess raffia strands and any excess round reed using a craft knife.

BASKET REED

Basket reed is made from any of a number of species of thorny, vine-like palms that grow from southern China to Australia and that are also found in Fiji, West Africa, and Madagascar. Known primarily as rattan (genera *Calamus* and *Daemonorops*), processed parts of this plant are used for furniture making, wicker-type work, and basketry. The horizontal stems of the rattan plant can grow up to 650 feet (200 meters) long.

The outside layer of rattan vine is used to create caning reeds, commonly used in chair seat weaving or for spoke basket rim binders. Cane or caning reeds are used to lash extra material around the rim of a basket. That extra material protects and hides the ends of the turned spokes in round basketry work or in rib baskets to add an accent vine to the rim hoop. In rib basket construction, cane can be used for both the ear pattern and as weavers.

The inner section of the rattan vine is cut and shaped to become the weaving reeds (weavers). Reed is identified by shape, thickness, and use within the basket construction. The spokes of your rib basket are most often made using the larger sizes of round reed or half-round reed, from size #3 through size #8. The weavers can be flat, flat oval, and oval oval, but also round. Basket reed, whether flat or round, is sold in rolled coils of 1 lb. (0.5kg).

Also available for weaving are splints, which are thin strips of oak, maple, ash, and even walnut that are typically ¼" to 3" (0.6 to 7.6cm) wide. Splints of larger widths, from ½" to ¾" (1.3 to 1.9cm) wide, are excellent for several of the simpler ear patterns.

Reed is sold in bundles.

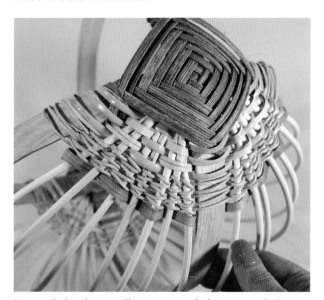

Most rib baskets will use several shapes and sizes of reed. In this sample, the God's Eye is worked in ¼" flat reed. The first rows of weaving are worked using 3mm cane, followed by #2 round reed and a single ¼" flat reed. (For more information about the different sizes, see page 24.)

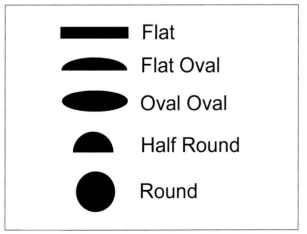

▬▬▬	Flat
⬬	Flat Oval
⬮	Oval Oval
◗	Half Round
●	Round

Cross-sections of the different reed shapes.

Handling Basket Reed

Open a reed coil carefully by cutting the strings or ribbons that bind the coil together. In general, the longest reeds will be on the inside of the coil or bundle and the shortest reeds on the outside. Short lengths are excellent for weaving just a few rows near the ear of a rib basket. Save the long inner lengths for filling in large areas on the sides of a basket or for more difficult weaving patterns where you want to avoid needing to add a new reed.

Remove several lengths of reed and roll them into small coils of individual reeds. Feed the end of each reed through the center of the coil several times to secure it. Smaller sizes of reed, whether flat or round, can easily be coiled into small circles around 5" (12.7cm) across without presoaking. Larger sizes may need to be coiled in 8" (20cm) or 10" (26cm) circles.

These small rolls are ready for the soaking pot. Recoil the unused reed bundle and tie it with a string. Store the coil in a small trash bag, keeping the bag open to allow airflow.

Flat and Round Basket Reed

Flat reed is sold in widths expressed in US inches (imperial measurement). Rib basketry commonly uses flat reed weavers from 3/16" to 1/2" (0.5 to 1.3cm) wide.

Round reed is sold under a numbering system; the larger the number, the larger the diameter of the reed. #00 is the smallest size, and #8 is the largest size commonly used for rib baskets.

In general, the longest reeds will be on the inside of the coil or bundle and the shortest reeds on the outside.

A Note on Metric Sizes

Throughout this book, metric equivalents are given for all measurements except for actual reed sizes. If you are a reader who uses the metric system, simply refer to the flat reed size table on this page to double-check which size reed to purchase or use.

Flat reed size (inches)	Approx. width in millimeters	Approx. feet per pound
11/64	4.4	410
3/16	4.8	400
1/4	6.4	370
7mm*	(0.275")	300
3/8	9.5	210
1/2	12	150
5/8	15.9	120
3/4	19.1	90

*This metric size is commonly sold by basketry suppliers.

Round reed size (designation #)	Approx. diameter in millimeters	Approx. diameter in inches	Approx. feet per pound
0	1.2	3/64	2,200
1	1.6	1/16	1,600
2	1.75	3/16	1,100
2.5	2	5/64	900
3	2.4	3/32	750
3.5	2.5	31/32	600
4	2.8	7/64	500
4.5	3.2	1/8	400
5	3.6	9/64	350
5.5	4.0	5/32	325
6	4.4	11/64	200
6.5	4.8	3/16	160
7	5.2	13/64	150
8	6.0	15/64	105
9	7.1	9/32	90

DRIED BOTANICALS AND NATURAL FIBERS

Just as they can be formed into hoops for your rims (see page 21), grapevine, honeysuckle, and wisteria vine, among other dried botanicals, can become the weavers of your basket design, adding texture and color to your work. The three materials listed can be purchased through basketry supply stores, and some can be harvested directly from your backyard, depending on where you live. In fact, the species of dried botanicals that were traditionally used in basketry depended on the artist's location. A basket maker who lived in the Appalachian Mountains, on the east coast of the United States, may have used wild grapevine, bark strips from the poplar tree, or splints of oak, ash, or maple. Along the Pacific Northwest, the main basket-weaving materials available would have been cedar bark, willow branches, and beargrass. The extra-long needles from the long-needled pine were often used in basketry in the American South.

If you want to harvest your own fresh botanicals for use in your basketwork, choose healthy, mature leaves or plant stems. Rinse the harvest in water mixed with a small amount of bleach to remove any insects or insect eggs. Gently rinse with clean water and then set on a clean towel to dry. Bundle the leaves or stems at the base with a string and hang upside down in a paper bag to protect the weaving material from sunlight and dust. Leave the bag slightly open to allow for air circulation. Place the bag in a dark, dry area and allow the plant material to dry completely before use.

Thickly stemmed natural weavers, like willow branches or wisteria vine, can take up to a year to dry thoroughly, but most finer branches and leaves will be ready to use in about one to two months. If the material feels cold to the touch of your cheek, that material is still damp. When the material held to your cheek has no temperature feeling, then all of the moisture in the plant has dried out.

The top coil is ¼" flat reed; the middle coil is ⅜" purple-dyed flat reed; under that is dried honeysuckle vine; and the bottom coil is dried wisteria vine.

Suggested Common Plants

- Alfalfa stems
- Bamboo sheaths
- Cattail leaves
- Clematis vine
- Corn husks
- Crownvetch stems
- Daylily leaves
- Honeysuckle vine
- Horsetail grass
- Japanese iris leaves
- Long-needled pine
- Pampas grass leaves and stems
- Sedge grass
- Tansy stems
- Virginia creeper vine
- Wheat stems
- Yucca leaves

Suggested Bark, Branches, and Splints

- Ash
- Black walnut
- Forsythia
- Maple
- Oak
- Poplar
- Willow

OTHER WEAVING MATERIALS

There is a wide variety of natural weaving materials available through your local craft or needle-arts store. Cord, thread, or yarn made from jute, cotton, wool, and even paper make wonderful, decorative weavers. You can use raffia, twine, cotton cord, and even wool yarn. Here are some ideas:

- Bamboo yarn
- Cotton crochet thread
- Cotton yarn
- Cut burlap strips

- Hemp twine
- Jute twine
- Loose wood fibers
- Raffia ribbon

- Rolled newsprint paper
- Twisted paper cords
- Wool yarn

Raffia, twine, cotton cord, and even wool yarn make colorful, textured additions to rib basket weaving.

WORKING WITH DIFFERENT WEAVING MATERIALS

Using different materials throughout your basketwork adds color, texture, and interest to even the simplest of weaves. Any weaving pattern can be worked in flat, flat oval, oval oval, or round reed, with each material creating its own unique look.

The variety of textures, thicknesses, and colors in this basket adds a lot of interest.

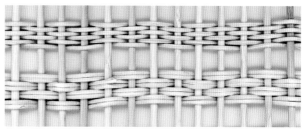

This simple weave, called "over one under one," is the most basic weaving pattern for rib baskets and is worked by weaving the reed (or other weaver) over one spoke and then under the next spoke. This sample is created using ¼" flat reed. You can see how uniform and repetitive the pattern looks.

Round reed creates a tightly packed woven surface. In this photo, the top sample is worked in the over one under one weaving pattern using one strand of round reed to create each finished row. The lower sample is worked in the same over one under one pattern using two strands per row.

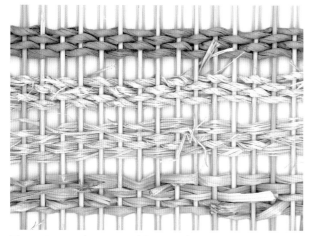

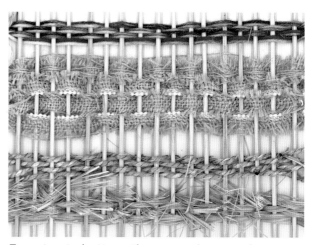

From top to bottom, this set of weaving samples are worked in chair rush cord, twisted raffia cord, loose raffia strands, and dried daylily leaves. All the samples are done using the over one under one weaving pattern. Note how different the texture of the weave becomes when you compare the carefully twisted chair rush cord to the loose raffia strands.

From top to bottom, these weaving samples are worked using paired strands of worsted weight wool yarn, cut burlap strips, 3mm twisted seagrass cord, and loose seagrass strands.

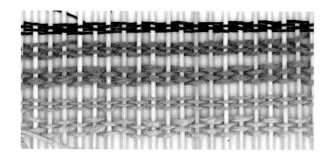

Many common natural fiber threads and twines work wonderfully as weavers. In this sample, from top to bottom, are black ⅛" (0.3cm) leather lacing, 3mm burlap twine, dyed jute twine, twisted paper cord, and common garden twine.

Dyes and Colors

DYEING REED WITH BASKET DYES

Basket dyes are available in powder and liquid form; powdered dyes are my favorite coloring agent to use. Any dye product that will color wood or fabric can be used to color rib baskets. Most packages of dye will color a 1 lb. (0.5kg) reed coil. Follow the manufacturer's instructions. You can buy specific colors and mix them together to create new shades for your reeds. You can also reuse the dye solution several times, dipping new coils into the color. The first coils will dye darker in tone than the later coils. This gives you a nice gradation of color from just one dye batch.

Before you begin, prepare your work area by covering it with old newspapers or a large trash bag. The basket dye will color anything it touches. Use latex gloves to avoid dyeing your hands. Most dyes require an aluminum pot for the solution. If you will be dyeing an entire reed coil, remove any strings or ribbons.

The subtle brown and vivid red shown here were both achieved with basket dyes.

1 Gently loosen the coil to allow the dye solution to reach into the deepest areas in the bundle. You can also pull out individual strands of reed to be dyed. Roll these reeds into small coils of five to six strands each. For powdered dyes, add the recommended amount of water to an aluminum pot and bring the water to a boil. Add the dye, stirring well with an aluminum spoon. Turn off the stove burner and move the pot onto a wooden cutting board.

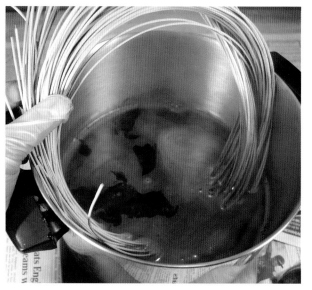

2 Using your metal spoon, lower the reed coils into the dye. For evenly coated, solid-colored strands, immerse the entire coil at once. You can dye several small coils at a time to create identical coloration for those strands. When the reeds have reached the desired color, remove the coil(s) from the dye bath. Allow the coil(s) to drip well over the pot and then move them onto a stack of newspapers to allow to dry.

3 Space-dye your reeds by dipping only half of the coil into the dye solution. After this area develops a dark color, roll the entire coil through the dye to apply a small amount of coloring to the remaining section of the reeds.

You can achieve a surprising variety of looks using dyes like this.

COLORING REED WITH ACRYLIC CRAFT PAINT

Acrylic craft paints can give your baskets bright, colorful tones that are permanent. When coloring reeds before weaving, thin the paint to allow the color to soak into the reeds uniformly according to the following instructions.

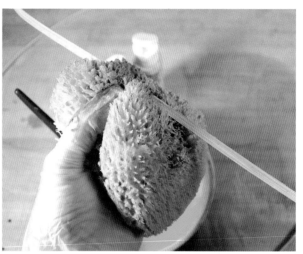

1 Thin the paint with about one tablespoon (15ml) of color to one cup (240ml) of water. This will allow the paint to totally saturate the reed.

2 Dip a large sea sponge into your thinned paint. Wrap the sponge around one end of the reed and slowly pull the reed through the paint-laden sponge. Allow the reed to dry completely. You can reapply color later to darken the tone.

Alternatively, to create a distressed color effect, use the paint directly from the bottle or jar on the finished basket. Brush one to two coats over the outside surface of the reeds. Allow the paint to dry completely, and then use 220-grit sandpaper to lightly sand the outer surface of the reeds. The sandpaper will lift the paint from the high areas of the weaving patterns, leaving the color where the reeds tuck under a spoke.

3 Dye or paint a few extra reeds whenever you are coloring. They will be ready for that moment of inspiration when you want a touch of color in your next project.

DYEING REED WITH POWDERED DRINK MIXES

While you will often dye individual reed strands to create small areas of color in a basket, you can also dye an entire basket one color after the weaving is complete.

This 5" (12.7cm) diameter wheel-ear basket was dyed using a powdered drink mix after all of the weaving steps were done. By dyeing the entire basket at once, you can ensure that the basket comes out with a consistent color throughout for each of your hoop, spoke, and weaving materials.

Note that different materials pick up color differently, though—for example, in this basket, the wooden hoops don't look the same as the reed weavers, and the braids of raffia hardly picked up the color at all. Any given basket is created from multiple plant fibers, and each material will absorb color at a different rate. Raffia may accept only a small amount of dye, while rattan reed will dye to a deep color tone.

The steps for dyeing with this method are simple. Mix one packet of powdered drink mix with one quart (950ml) of warm water for light colors, or use two packets per quart for stronger colors. Stir well. Wearing latex gloves, roll the basket in the solution until every area of the basket is wet. Remove the basket from the mix and allow to drip dry for about ten minutes. Repeat until the basket is the desired color. Allow to dry thoroughly.

Finishes, Repairs, and Care

MAKING REPAIRS

Repair any breaks in older baskets by cleaning the basket with oil soap or a light solution of bleach and water. Dampen a short length of reed that matches the broken weaver in size. Tuck the new reed under a spoke two to three spaces away from the break. Weave the new reed through the spokes, going over the older reed. Cut and tuck the end of the new reed under a spoke two to three spaces from the break on its other side.

CLEANING

The small melon basket shown below has seen years of use as one of my garden tool baskets. Over time, it naturally picks up dirt, dust, mildew, and even fungus. So, once a year, I clean this basket and all my other handcrafted baskets in either a bleach and water solution or an oil soap solution. For either cleaning method, use a large bucket or your bathtub or, if you prefer, work outdoors in a wheelbarrow.

Bleach and Water

Create a mild bleach and water mixture. For my bathtub or wheelbarrow, I pour 3 cups (700ml) of bleach (I use Clorox®) into a half-filled tub. Wearing heavy latex gloves, dip the basket into the solution

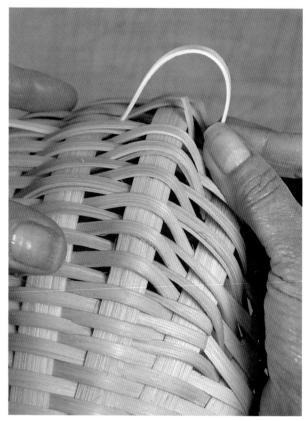

A short length of new reed can fix a broken reed.

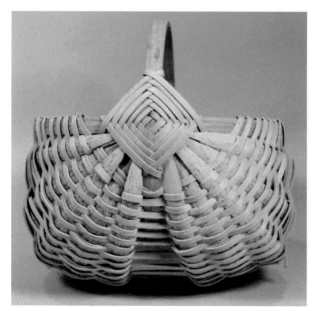

A hardworking basket before cleaning.

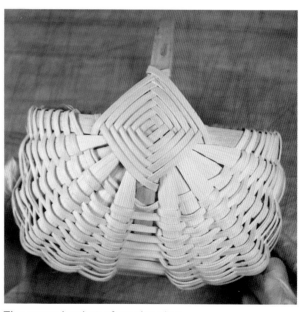

The same basket after cleaning.

and, with a soft-bristled kitchen brush, clean your basket inside and out. Remove the basket from the solution and shake well to eliminate the excess water. Rinse in clean water and, again, shake well. Gently reshape the basket if necessary. Let the basket dry well in your bathtub if you are cleaning inside or in the shade if you are working outdoors. A cleaning like this will remove most stains, dirt spots, and markings left from mildew.

Oil Soap

The oil soaps that are used to clean old furniture or used as leather saddle soap work wonderfully to clean both newly made reed baskets and any antique baskets that you have collected. This product cleans the dirt from the baskets without bleaching the beautiful natural patina that old baskets develop over time. To use, follow the manufacturer's instructions.

FINISHING WITH SEALERS

You can leave a completed basket unfinished. Traditionally, most baskets are left in their natural state—as raw reed. Alternatively, you can add a finishing coat, a sealer, to the reed to help protect the basket from dust, dirt, and humidity. Raw reed has a dull, matte tone, and sealers come in high gloss, gloss, satin, and matte, so you can choose the effect you would like.

I always use a sealer on decorative baskets. The sealer adds a touch of sparkle and helps make the basket easy to clean with just a dusting brush or dry cloth. If the basket is a working basket—such as an egg basket or a basket for carrying garden tools—then I leave the basket in its raw reed state.

Oils

Danish oil, tung oil, and mineral oil can be applied to your baskets using a soft-bristled brush. Allow

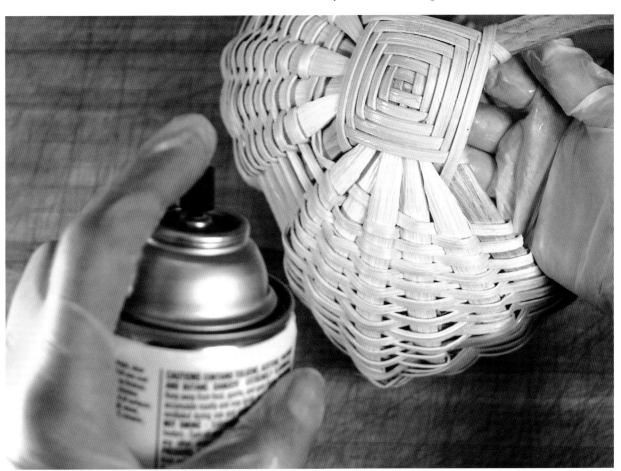

An advantage to any spray sealer is that the spray can penetrate into the deeper areas—the tucks—of your weaving.

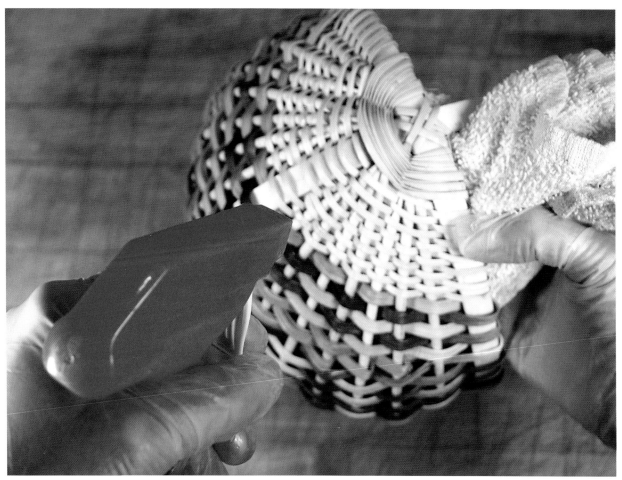

Spray oil finishes penetrate through the basket.

the oil coating to set for several minutes and then wipe off the excess oil. Oils brighten and deepen the natural color of the reed.

Spray Finish

Spray finishes, whether acrylic or polyurethane, are quick and easy to use. Simply follow the directions on the can. These sealers create a smooth, silky feeling to your baskets and help protect the baskets from water.

Brush-On Finish

Acrylic and polyurethane sealers are also available in brush-on formulas. Follow the manufacturer's instructions. Polyurethane brush-on sealer is especially excellent when you want to strengthen the reed of a basket. Baskets with wide spaces between spokes or that use natural materials harden with several coats of a polyurethane sealer.

Paste Wax

Paste wax can be applied using an old toothbrush to work the wax into the deeper areas of your basketry. Wax lends a soft, gentle feeling to the basket reed, along with a soft sheen.

Spray Oil Polish

Even spray polishes can be used to add a little shine to your reed. Build the polish up by working several light coats, buffing with a dry, clean cloth between each coat. Don't forget to oil the inside as well as the outside.

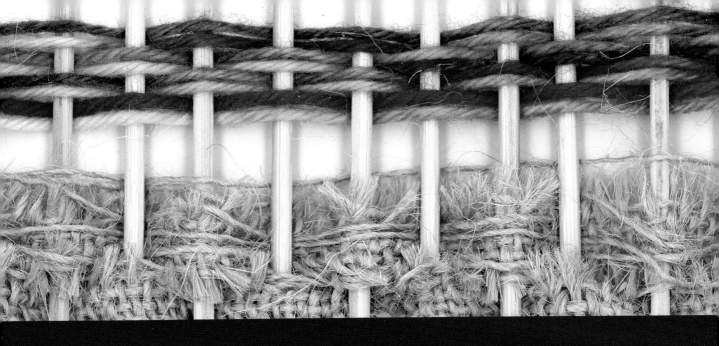

CHAPTER 2

TECHNIQUES

Common Rib Basket Shapes and Basket Names

Rib baskets are more often identified by the shape of the central bottom area and the slope of the sides than by their intended use. Different body shapes have different names. The naming of a basket can also change according to the region and time period in which it was created.

Shape and naming are two different aspects. Shape is determined by the size, positioning, and placement of the spokes off the joining ear. The name is determined by the shape, usage, and specific features of the basket, as well as the area of the country in which it was first designed.

Many of the crafts, hobbies, and arts that we enjoy have well-defined, standardized terminology for the different tools, techniques, and parts of that craft. For example, a knitting pattern has a strict, unchangeable terminology and description to create specific stitch patterns that can be exactly reproduced. Classic Old World woodcarving uses a strict series of tools, cuts, and strokes to create iconic images. Rib basketry, however, has no standardized, strict set of rules because it was a fireside homestead craft taught by one generation to the next. Because this craft was passed on by family lines in isolated communities, what one region of the country might call an egg basket could be called a twin bottom basket in another.

So one basic rib basket design might be called a split bottom, twin bottom, or shallow fanny basket. All these basket shapes have a shallow indent in the profile at the bottom point of the spine. That same basket can also be called an egg basket, pickle basket,

This single basket could have many names.

The name of a rib basket is sometimes based on the basket's function, like this egg basket.

or feed basket because each region tended to create a particular basket design for a specific use around the homestead.

The overall size of the rib basket can also influence the name given to the basket. Egg baskets tend to be small, around 6" to 8" (15 to 20cm) wide at the rim. This was because the youngest child on the homestead often had the chore of collecting the eggs and therefore could only carry a small basket.

Fanny baskets use the same low or shallow indent at the bottom spine, dividing the basket into two split sides. They are about the size and profile of a woman's "fanny" (backside) as she is bent hoeing in the garden. Fanny baskets are larger than egg baskets, usually measuring around 12" to 18" (30 to 45cm) across the rim hoop. The shallow split bottom of the large fanny basket makes it perfect for harvesting potatoes, onions, and tomatoes without damage. The low indent at the spine keeps the fruits or vegetables from rolling around inside the basket, yet the basket is easy to drag across garden rows without getting snagged on rocks, roots, and vines.

A hip basket is often the largest of the rib basket varieties, with a very deep indent at the bottom spine. This deep indent allows the basket to rest on your hipbone with the split bottom sides balanced on either side of that resting point. Being able to carry the basket on your hip means that you can carry a heavier load or harvest. Therefore, the hip basket is a favorite for picking apples or squash or carrying grain.

So, the **name** of your rib basket can be determined by:
- The shape of the basket profile
- The primary use of the basket design
- The region in which the design originated
- The depth of the basket walls
- Whether or not the basket has a hoop handle, side handles, or no handle

Note: Don't get too sidetracked with learning to name or identify different baskets "properly."

The actual **physical shape** of your rib basket is determined by three main factors:
- The shape of the rim hoop—whether you use a round, oval, or rounded rectangle hoop
- The length of each spoke, which creates the curvature of the profile of the basket at the spine
- The placement of each spoke

As you manipulate these factors in your design, you determine the shape of the basket at the rim, the shape of the side walls, and the depth of the split of the bottom (if applicable) along the spine or below the handle. Handle and rim differences also play a part in determining the overall final appearance of the basket.

BODY SHAPES

Remember: as described previously, names for different baskets vary widely. But here is a quick tour through some common shapes you will encounter and some ways you can refer to them.

Classic Egg Baskets

The graduated lengths of the side spokes in a classic egg basket divide the bottom area of the basket into two separate sections, with the bottom of each section lower than the spine. When our great-grandmothers, as children, went to collect the eggs from the henhouse, they would place each egg in one or the other sides of the bottom of the basket. Because of the split and because of the natural bowl shape on each side, the eggs could not roll and therefore could not break.

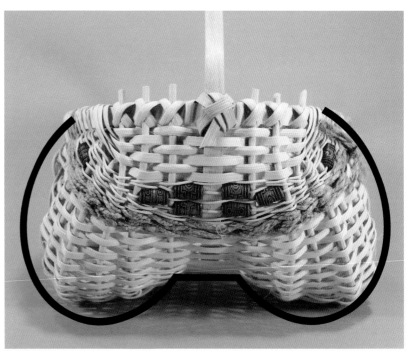

This classic egg basket has a medium-depth split at the spine, with the longest spokes falling at a low middle point on each side curve.

Twin Bottom Baskets

The twin bottom or split bottom egg basket—other common names for the classic egg design—also uses spokes that are slightly longer than the spine. This style does not have the more obvious split of the classic egg basket but still creates two separate bowls at the bottom of the basket. In the end, classic egg baskets and twin bottom baskets are essentially the same thing, with some variations in exact shape as shown between the photos.

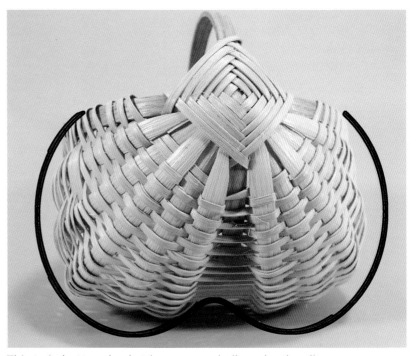

This twin bottom basket has a very shallow-depth split.

Oval Fanny Baskets

The oval fanny basket uses an oval rim hoop (rather than round or any other shape), which is where the name comes from. The term "fanny" refers to splitting the bottom into two separate areas by using bottom spokes that are slightly longer than the spine, as in the classic egg basket and twin bottom basket. The use of the oval rim hoop allows the basket maker to create a wider basket that will balance well when carried on the hipbone.

The term "fanny basket" comes from the obvious double buttock shape of the basket bottom. This style of basket can also be called a hip basket. The shallow divide between the two bottom sides of the basket allows the carrier to position that center divide comfortably on the hipbone, which allows for carrying much heavier weights in larger baskets than might be possible if using just a handle. There are several different oval fanny basket styles, including deep, long, and shallow, as you can see in the photos.

This long oval fanny basket uses the oval rim hoop for only the inner half of the wall weaving. The spokes are cut much longer than the rim hoop, which pushes the sides away from the far edges of the rim hoop. A long fanny basket doesn't necessarily have to have this rim gap (side handles).

Combining both the gradually longer spokes of a deep oval fanny basket and the extra-long spokes of the long oval fanny basket, this shallow fanny basket is ready to take to the potato patch. "Shallow" here refers to the depth of the bottom divide, not to the actual depth of the overall basket.

This deep oval fanny basket used the placement of the rim hoop relative to the handle hoop (it is set high up on the handle hoop) and a set of gradually lengthening spokes to make the height of the basket sides much longer than its width.

Full Fanny/Full Hip Baskets

By dramatically lengthening the bottom spokes beyond the length of the spine, you can create a full fanny basket. The division area along the spine is used to rest the basket on the user's hipbone.

When you design your own full fanny basket, begin by deciding how deep the spine will be—that is, where the rim will sit relative to the handle and therefore how much of the handle hoop will serve as the spine. Knowing how deep the spine will be will determine how long your longest spokes must be cut, because they have to be dramatically longer than the spine. The longest spokes are placed below the center point of the ear on each side of the basket. In this sample, the longest spokes are clearly the ones where the basket bottom touches the table. All other spokes are then cut to gradually taper in size toward the rim hoop or the spine.

Oriole Baskets

An oriole basket is named for its curvature, which is reminiscent of the hanging nest of a Baltimore oriole. The inward curve of the top walls of an oriole basket are created by cutting the top spokes slightly smaller than one-half of the rim hoop size. The tight spoke area continues until about one-third of the way down the side wall, where the basket sides begin to flare out beyond the diameter of the rim hoop.

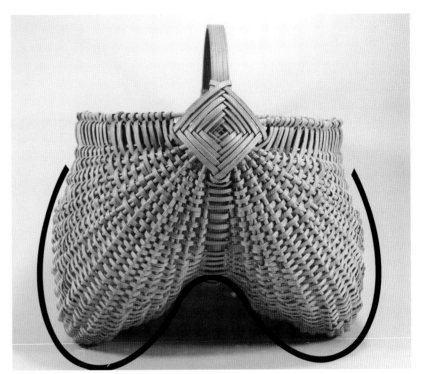

This full fanny or full hip basket has a dramatically deep divide between the two separate bottoms of the design. The spine stands nearly 3″ (7.6cm) off the table in this extra-large work.

The free-floating (partially unwoven) spokes that radiate from the half God's Eye—one above the rim hoop and two that drop below the center point of the wall sides—make this oriole basket into an art rib oriole basket.

Melon Baskets

By using spoke lengths that match or nearly match one-half of the rim hoop length, you can create half-sphere basket sides, commonly called melon baskets. There is a wide range of basket shapes that fall under the general category of melon baskets. A melon basket has a very round or semi-round bottom that does not divide at the bottom of the basket into two separate bowls like all of the previously described baskets do. The lowest point in the basket instead falls along the central spine formed from the handle hoop.

True melon baskets—those with well-rounded bottoms—tend to rock rather than sitting steadily. As shown in the photos, a true melon basket might perch in just about any position anywhere along its bottom and sides.

This melon basket uses spokes that all match the length of one-half of the rim hoop. As the spokes radiate out from the ear in evenly spaced positions, the final shape of the basket becomes a half-sphere.

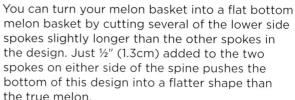

You can turn your melon basket into a flat bottom melon basket by cutting several of the lower side spokes slightly longer than the other spokes in the design. Just ½" (1.3cm) added to the two spokes on either side of the spine pushes the bottom of this design into a flatter shape than the true melon.

Using spokes that are slightly longer than one-half of the rim hoop pushes the sides of the melon basket out, making the basket appear bottom heavy. This can be called a low round melon basket.

HANDLE OPTIONS

Small and medium rib baskets often use a wooden hoop as the handle. You can also use coils of grapevine, kudzu, and even willow branches to create decorative handle hoops. Larger baskets meant to carry more weight might omit the handle due to weight limitations. Here are three primary options you'll encounter.

This simple melon basket uses a ½" (1.3cm) wide, 6" (15.2cm) diameter embroidery hoop to create both the spine of the basket and the handle.

Deer antlers, driftwood, and curly willow sticks make great flat handles for your rib baskets. A flat handle lies parallel or curves only slightly above the rim hoop. In this art rib oriole basket (the same as the one pictured on page 41), the driftwood branch is lashed to the rim in three places—once on the thick end of the branch and twice where the branch splits into two on the other end.

Traditional potato basket designs, such as this one, drop the weaving from the rim hoop to the first spoke about 4" (10.2cm) from the half God's Eye knot. This exposes a large area of the rim hoop, effectively making that area into side handles.

Common Rib Basket Shapes and Basket Names ■ **43**

RIM OPTIONS

The rim hoop of your rib basket can be used to accent the texture, size, and color of your weaving reeds. To protect the weaving reeds where they wrap over the rim hoop, consider adding a rim covering of yucca or cornhusks. The rim area of your basket is a wonderful area to accent your design elements.

TECHNIQUES

Create a rim hoop cover by lashing bamboo sheaths, cornhusks, pampas grass leaves, or yucca leaves over the rim using loose raffia strands.

This large hip potato basket, with its wide rim, shows off the three central spokes (forming the spine), the diagonal movement of the five-point lashing, the straight wrap of the over one under one weave, and the use of one extra-large weaver.

This small grape basket was woven with an open side rim handle. After the weaving steps were complete, several strands of fine, dried grape were soaked in warm water for fifteen minutes until they were pliable. The grapevines were then lashed to both the rim hoop and the top spoke of the side handles using #1 round reed.

Making Ears, Eyes, and Knots

Ears and eyes are lashing patterns used to bind two hoops together, such as one hoop that will become the handle and one hoop that will become the rim, or to create a weave on the intersection of rim and handle that can receive new spokes. The terms "ear," "eye," and "knot" are often used interchangeably. Multiple ear patterns can be combined in one basket. Sometimes you may have a simple ear that secures the handle hoop to the rim hoop, and then you might weave an eye design on top of it. In this book, we will use the general term "ear" to refer to any weaving pattern that lashes two frame pieces together, and we will use the term "eye" only when the specific pattern is a type of eye

shape, such as the God's Eye pattern (page 53). So, effectively, the God's Eye is an ear!

After looking over the examples shown here, you'll find the following pages full of different ear-weaving patterns (or simply "ears") that you can use as desired in your baskets. The selection is large and varied, meaning that you can achieve a wide variety of possibilities in your basket making! You can decide to use whatever ear suits your project; just refer back to these pages as needed.

Which ear pattern you choose for your basket designs will vary according to how the basket will be used and which elements of your basket you wish to emphasize. A full God's Eye ear creates a

TECHNIQUES

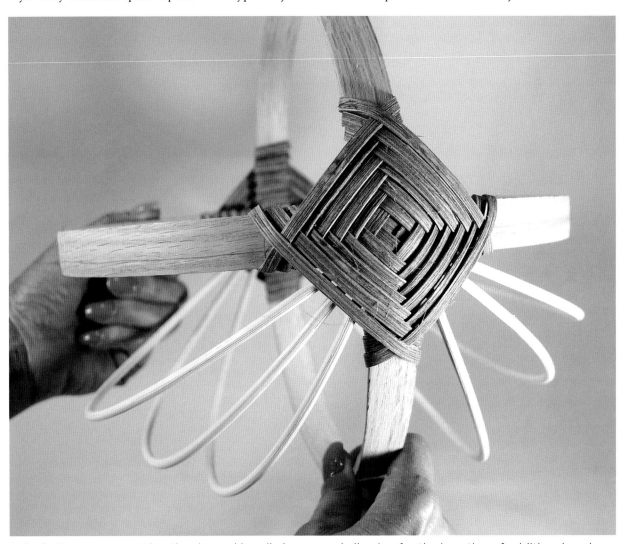

A God's Eye ear connecting the rim and handle hoops and allowing for the insertion of additional spokes.

bold, obvious design element at the handle joint—perfect for a decorative fireside basket. But that same God's Eye ear is too exposed and worked with very narrow reed that will not stand up to hard use in the orchard. For an orchard basket, then, instead consider using a double X ear made with wider flat reed.

Of all of the ear, eye, and knot patterns, the half God's Eye is an essential technique for the new basket maker, as this ear is often needed in combination with other smaller ear patterns to create the space that will anchor the first set of spokes.

This God's Eye ear may be the most recognized hoop-securing ear pattern used in rib basketry. It is easy to weave, creates a large area to secure your spokes, and becomes a visual focal point. But it is just one of a wide range of ear options available to the basket maker. See page 53 for instructions.

The double X ear shown here, worked in ¼" (0.6cm) maple splint, is strong enough to bind the handle and rim hoops into place. In this sample, the ear pattern is dramatically minimized. See page 47 for instructions.

This basket combines a God's Eye ear with a half God's Eye ear to secure the two hoops and create the space for spoke insertion. This combination ear is worked in paired #1 round reed. See page 75 for instructions.

TECHNIQUES

The double X ear pattern locks the two hoops—the handle and rim—tightly while taking up little space in the weaving area of the design. This ear is often worked in larger flat reed sizes, from ½" to 1" wide. This sample is woven with ⅜" flat reed over two ½" (1.3cm) hoops.

1 Set the rim hoop over the handle hoop, centering the hoop intersection on both sides of the basket. Place a flat reed to the back of the hoop intersection, with the working length to the upper left.

2 Holding the end of the reed on the back of the hoops, bring the working end over the upper left corner and down to the lower right.

TECHNIQUES

3 Bring the weaver around to the inside of the hoops and then up, returning it to its original position in the upper left.

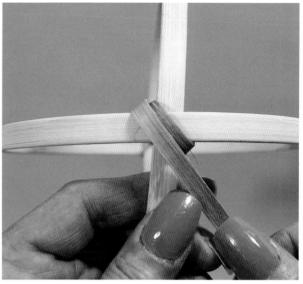

4 Bring the weaver to the front and back down to the lower right as you did in step 2. You have now wrapped the weaver twice over this area in this direction.

5 Bring the weaver back behind the lower section of the handle hoop to place it in back of the lower left.

6 Bring the weaver to the front of the basket and up to cross the intersection to place the reed in the upper right.

7 Return the weaver to the back of the lower left by folding it down along the back of the intersection.

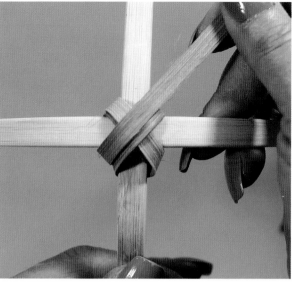

8 Bring the weaver up over the front of the intersection to the upper right again. You have now wrapped the weaver twice over this area in this direction.

9 Turn your work so that the inside of the ear area is facing you.

10 With a packing tool, open a channel under the ear (on the inside of the hoops) from the bottom of the knot to the top.

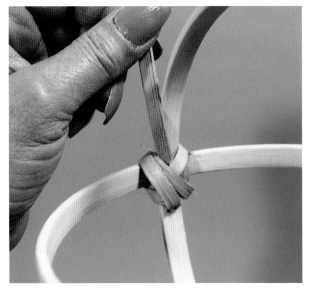

11 Insert the end of the weaver into the channel from bottom to top, then pull the weaver tight. It is often easier to work this step after first clipping the excess weaver to about 8" (20cm) long.

12 With a bench knife or craft knife, trim any excess weaver that shows above the inside of the knot.

DOUBLE BOW

The double bow ear is worked in smaller widths of flat reed. In this sample, the ear is worked in ¼" (0.6cm) oak splint over two ½" (1.3cm) hoops, but we'll call it a reed for the sake of simplicity—you can of course use reed. Like the double X, this design is often used in combination with the half God's Eye ear design. This ear is worked counterclockwise.

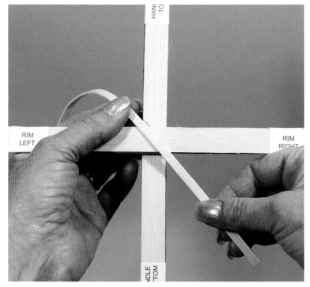

1 Hold one end of the reed in front of the hoop intersection, along one diagonal, with the working length of the reed above the rim hoop. Allow a 4"–5" (10–12cm) tail.

2 Fold the reed down behind the left rim hoop. Bring the reed up across the second diagonal so that the reed is now above the rim hoop on the opposite side (the upper right).

3 Fold the reed behind the top handle hoop horizontally to the top left. Then bring the reed down across the same diagonal as the first (in step 1).

4 Fold the reed up behind the right rim hoop, then diagonally down across the front again. Then fold it behind the bottom handle hoop horizontally to the lower right.

5 Bring the reed up across the front diagonally one more time, making sure the original tail stays in the bottommost position.

6 Fold the reed back behind the left rim hoop and clamp in place on the rim hoop.

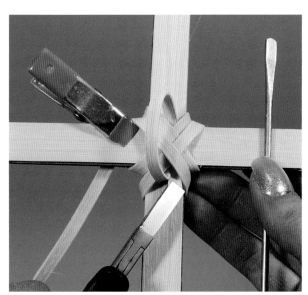

7 Bring the reed tail up over the knot, then tuck it down inside the top of the knot, threading it all the way through to the bottom of the knot.

8 Gently pull the tail to secure the knot, making the tail loop totally flat against the rest of the knot. Clip the tail, allowing about ½" (1.3cm) to show below the knot.

9 Turn the piece over. Unclamp and thread the working reed end down through the loop that is on the rim right below it. Clip the excess.

10 The completed double bow secures the two hoops and protects the knot reed intersection with the last tucked loop.

GOD'S EYE

The God's Eye is the iconic rib basket ear and is worked to bind the handle and rim hoop as well as to create a wide woven space in which to secure the spokes. A God's Eye is worked in a counterclockwise pattern. This sample is woven with ¼" flat reed over two ½" (1.3cm) hoops.

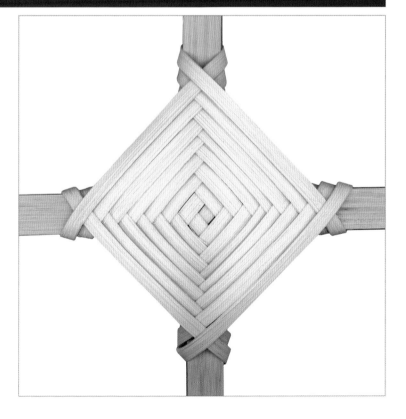

1 Tuck one end of your reed between the two hoops from the top left, sandwiching it in place. Bring the reed down across the diagonal to the lower right. Fold the reed back behind the bottom handle hoop to the lower left.

2 Bring the reed up across the diagonal to the upper right.

3 Fold the reed down behind the right rim hoop, then bring it diagonally across to the upper left.

4 Fold the weaver back behind the upper handle hoop and then bring it down diagonally across the front to the lower left.

5 Fold the reed up behind the left side rim. This completes one full round of the God's Eye pattern. In this photo, the reed has already then been brought back down diagonally across the front to the lower right, which is the beginning of the next full round.

6 Continue working in this four-step pattern for as many rounds as you desire. The larger the number of rounds, the larger the space you create to anchor your spokes. This photo shows about halfway through the second round.

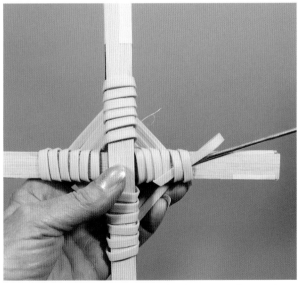

7 Use a packing tool to carefully adjust the position of the inner bars of the God's Eye. This knot has an indented look, with each new round rising above the last round.

8 Complete your weaving by bringing the reed to the inside of the basket after the last hoop loop. Use your packing tool to lift several loops on the rim, then tuck the end of the reed through the loops. Pull tight and clip the excess.

By lacing the reed through the previous loops of the God's Eye pattern, you can create a braided look with the outer rounds of the eye. Braided God's Eye ears really show the interlacing when you use reeds of smaller width. This sample uses 2.5mm cane worked over two ½" (1.3cm) hoops.

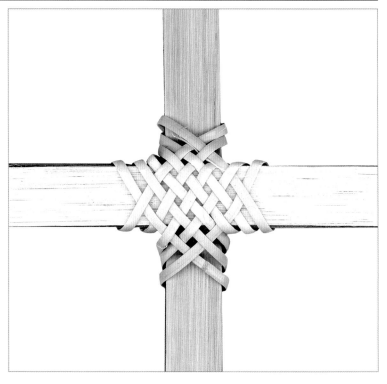

1 Following the directions for the God's Eye pattern (page 53), work one full round of weaving. Stop with the working end in the upper left.

2 Begin with a second round in the God's Eye pattern, but this time, as you bring the reed across the front, feed the end under the first loop of the weave it is crossing over (on the lower left), then over the second loop. This begins an under one over one weaving pattern. The pattern will change to over one under one (O1U1) as you proceed; it's just this first pass that is under one over one (starting with under instead of over).

3 Fold the reed back behind the lower handle hoop to the lower left. Bring the reed across the front to the top right, but lace the weaver over one loop, under one loop, and then over one loop of the weaving pattern already worked.

4 Repeat step 3 with the next pass of the pattern: fold the reed back behind the rim hoop down to the lower right, then bring it across the front to the top left, working the reed over one loop, under one loop, and over the third loop.

5 Continue in the counterclockwise God's Eye pattern, weaving the reed in an over one under one pattern at each pass. When you have worked your braided God's Eye to the desired size, secure the end of the reed by tucking under the reed on the inside of the basket. Pull tight and clip the end.

This simple and quick ear is worked in a figure-eight pattern, looping the two sides of the rim to the top and bottom of the handle hoop. Worked in ¼" flat reed over two ½" (1.3cm) hoops, this pattern develops a thick, three-dimensional ear that extends well beyond the walls of your basket.

1 Begin with the end of the reed held onto the center of the hoop intersection with its working end toward the upper left. Fold the reed horizontally behind the top handle hoop, then bring it down diagonally across to the lower left.

2 Fold the reed back behind the bottom handle hoop horizontally and then bring it up across the front diagonally to the upper left. This two-step process (steps 1 and 2) creates the basic figure-eight pattern of the ear.

3 Repeat steps 1 and 2 to create a new figure eight. Place each new lower loop (at the bottom of the figure eight) below the loop previously made. This elongates the bottom section of the ear to create the space on either side of the bottom handle hoop to receive spokes.

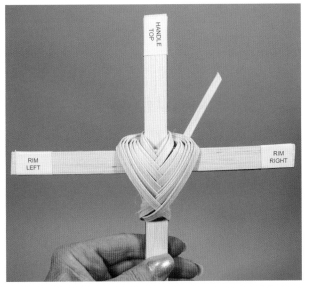

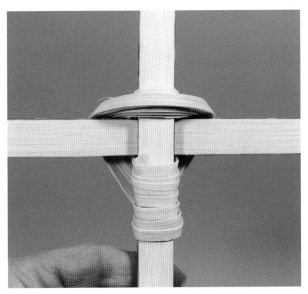

4 Work each new upper loop (at the top of the figure eight) directly on top of the previous loop. This stacks the loops to create a thick collar effect (see photo for step 5). From the inside of the basket, the collar acts like a shelf under which you can secure an above-the-rim spoke.

5 To finish the pattern, turn the piece to the back side (inside) and bring the reed up underneath all of the wrapped reeds on the bottom handle hoop.

The finished sample three-point lashing is worked in ¼" flat reed, but the step-by-step lashing was done using 2.5mm cane. Both were worked on two ½" (1.3cm) hoops. When finished, this lashing lies closer to the hoops than the two-point lashing with collar but makes a smaller spoke wall. This is a three-point lashing because there is no weaving around the upper handle hoop.

TECHNIQUES

1 Sandwich your reed between the two hoops at the intersection so that the reed extends from the top left. Bring the reed down across the intersection diagonally to the lower right.

2 Fold the reed back behind the lower handle hoop horizontally to the lower left. Then bring it up across the front of the hoops diagonally to the upper right.

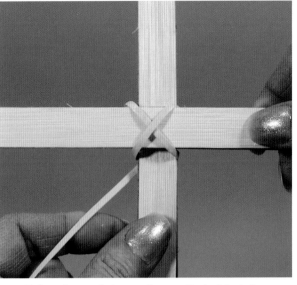

3 Bring the reed down diagonally behind the intersection to the lower left.

4 Fold the reed over and across the lower handle hoop horizontally, creating a bar on the front.

5 Bring the reed up diagonally behind the intersection to the upper left.

6 Repeat steps 1–5 until you have woven the ear to your desired size. With each full round, make sure you are wrapping slightly farther along the hoops, not directly on top of the previous wrap, in order to create the intended shape.

7 Secure the excess reed by turning the piece to the back side (inside) and tucking it up under several loops on the bottom handle hoop. Clip the extra length.

HALF GOD'S EYE

The half God's Eye is a three-point lashing that creates a place to anchor your spokes and that is worked on the rim hoop and bottom portion of the handle hoop, much like the three-point lashing (page 60). This may be the second most common ear weaving, after the God's Eye, used in rib basketry. This pattern makes a loop just under the rim hoop, a twisted V area, and a second loop next to the bottom handle hoop. Spokes can be inserted into either or both loops as well as into the twisted V area by opening a hole in the area using an awl. This sample was worked over two ½" (1.3cm) hoops using ¼" flat reed. A half God's Eye can be worked using smaller-width flat reed, small-diameter round reed, or cane. You can even create it by using two strands of small-diameter round reed as if they are one, called pairing.

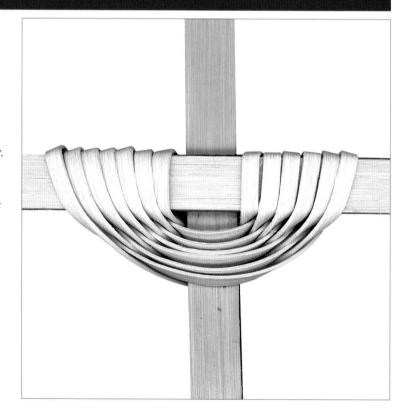

1 Begin by sandwiching the end of the reed between the two hoops, with the working end toward the upper left.

2 Fold the reed vertically down over the rim hoop as close to the handle hoop as possible. Give the reed a quarter twist to smoothly lay it back behind the bottom handle hoop horizontally. Refer to the photo to make sure you have done the quarter turn correctly.

3 Give the reed another quarter twist to fold it vertically up over the rim hoop as close to the handle hoop as possible, but this time on the right side. Refer to the photo to make sure you have done the quarter twist correctly. Fold the reed vertically down and back behind the rim hoop.

4 Give the reed a quarter twist and fold it horizontally across the bottom handle hoop, allowing it to follow the curve of the twisted reed in the corners. Give the reed another quarter twist and fold it up vertically behind the rim hoop on the left side, bringing it to the upper left.

5 Repeat this pattern, steps 2–4, to do another full round. With each full round, set the reed a little farther out along the hoops, not directly on top of the previous round.

6 Continue weaving full rounds until you have worked the ear to your desired thickness.

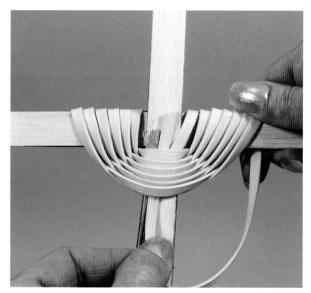

7 To secure the end of the reed, turn the piece to the back side (inside) and use a packing tool to open the space between the loops and the bottom handle hoop. Thread the end of the reed up from the bottom of the loops to the top. Pull the extra weaver tight through the loops and clip the excess.

8 While you have your packing tool in your hand, turn the piece back around to the front side (outside) and use the edge of the tool to straighten the front V created by the crossing twists of the weavers.

This ear is used to secure central spokes (acting as the spine) to your rim hoop when a handle hoop is not being used. The X pattern holds the spokes in place while the secondary weaving pattern of over one under one creates the spaces for the side spokes. This sample was worked over a ½" (1.3cm) hoop and #4 round reed spokes, using 3mm cane for the weaving. This is not shown in the photos, but you can cut a small slice, ¼" to ½" (0.6 to 1.3cm), from each end of the spoke to help lock the spokes flatly against the rim hoop.

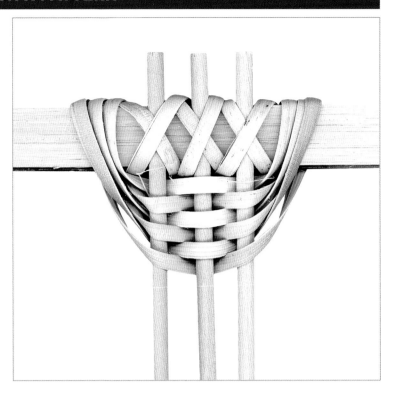

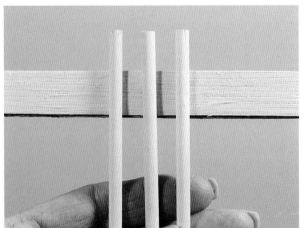

1 Position the spokes on the outside of the rim hoop, spaced approximately ½" (1.3cm) apart.

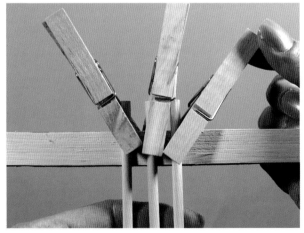

2 Optional: In my day-to-day basketwork, I use yellow wood glue to help secure the spokes in position while I am working an ear pattern. The glue is only temporary. If you want to use glue, measure your rim hoop and mark the position of each spoke. Use just one or two drops of wood glue on the back of each spoke, place the spokes into position, and clamp. Let the glue dry for several hours. Repeat for the other end of the spokes on the opposite side of the rim hoop. Do not use glue on a basket that you wish to enter in competitions.

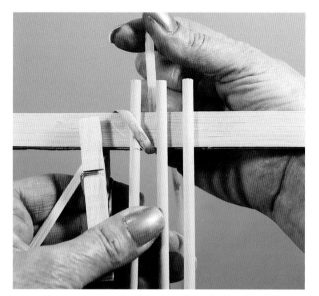

3 Clamp one end of the reed to the back of the left side rim hoop, leaving a 4"–6" (10–15cm) tail that you can tuck into the weaving pattern after the lashing is done. Bring the reed over the top of the rim and across the first spoke diagonally. Bring the reed up vertically on the back side between the first and second spoke.

4 Repeat the same diagonal cross described in step 3 for the remaining two spokes, ending with the reed on the back side of the rim at the upper right.

5 Repeat the same diagonal crosses, but reversed, in order to cross each spoke on the diagonal in the opposite direction, creating the X pattern. End with the reed on the back side of the rim at the upper left. This X pattern holds the spokes tightly against the rim hoop.

6 Get ready for the next part of the design by folding the reed down vertically across the front of the rim, ending with it at the lower left.

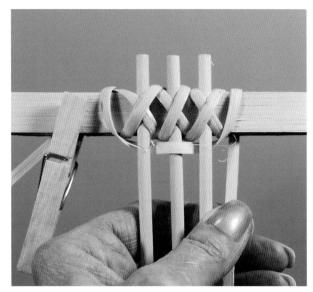

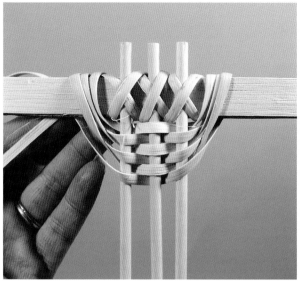

7 Give the reed a quarter twist and then weave it under the first spoke, over the second spoke, and under the third spoke, making sure the reed is flat against the second spoke as shown. Give the reed another quarter twist and fold it up vertically over the rim hoop. Get ready for the next pass by folding the reed down vertically behind the rim hoop again, ending with it at the lower right.

8 This pattern becomes a sort of modified half God's Eye with an over one under one weaving pattern worked over the center spokes, alternating between starting with over or under to achieve the pattern shown. Continue weaving until you have worked the ear to the desired size. Secure the two ends of the reed by tucking them under the loops on the inside of the basket.

THREE-SPOKE LASHING WITH BAR PATTERN

Where the X pattern in the previous ear was worked on the front of the basket, over the rim hoop, in this ear the X pattern is worked on the inside of the hoop, lacing the weaver over the top and bottom areas of the spokes to create the bar effect. This sample was worked over a ½" (1.3cm) hoop and #4 round reed spokes, using 3mm cane for the weaving.

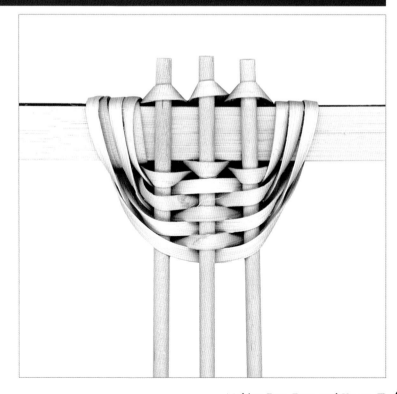

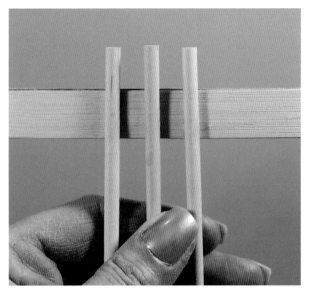

1 Position the spokes on the outside of the rim hoop, spaced approximately ½" (1.3cm) apart.

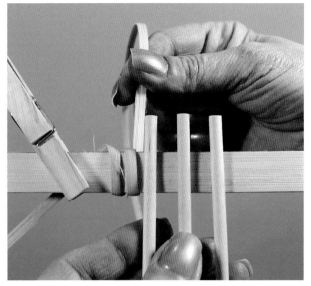

2 Clamp one end of the reed to the back of the left side rim hoop, leaving a 4"–6" (10–15cm) tail that you can tuck into the weaving pattern after the lashing is done. Fold the weaver down twice around the rim hoop, working from the top of the hoop and moving to the back at the bottom of the hoop.

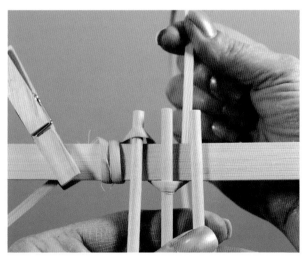

3 With the reed on the back side (inside) of the work, create a bar by twisting the reed and bringing it over the top of the first spoke where it extends above the rim hoop. Then bring the reed down vertically behind the rim hoop between the first and second spokes. Again create a bar by twisting the reed and bringing it over the top of the middle spoke where it extends below the rim hoop. Bring the reed up vertically behind the rim hoop between the middle and third spokes.

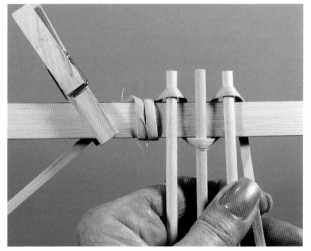

4 Create a third bar by twisting the reed and bringing it over the top of the third spoke where it extends above the rim hoop. End this bar sequence by bringing the reed down vertically behind the rim hoop beside the third spoke.

5 Begin wrapping bars across the unworked spoke areas by reversing the weave.

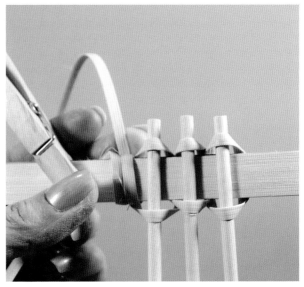

6 When this reverse pass is complete, all spokes will be bound to the rim with a weaver bar, and your reed will be back at the beginning position.

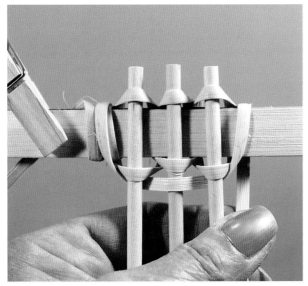

7 Working directly on top of the first two loops of the reed on the left side rim hoop, begin working the reed in the same pattern as the lower area of the three-spoke lashing with X pattern, working a quarter twist in the corner between the hoop and the end spokes (steps 7–8, page 67).

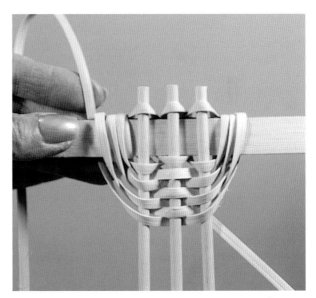

8 Complete this ear by securing the ends of the reed under several loops on the inside of the basket.

Worked in the same lashing and weaving pattern as the three-spoke lashing with X pattern ear, this pattern allows for unevenly spaced spokes and for air space—unworked space—between the X lashing pattern and the over one under one weaving pattern. This sample is worked over one ½" (1.3cm) hoop and #4 round reed spokes, using 2.5mm cane.

1 Determine the spacing that you want between the spokes and mark with a pencil. For my sample, I allowed twice as much space on either side of the center spoke as I used between all of the other spokes. This extra-wide spacing can become a place where you can split your fingers under the rim hoop as a handle. Position the spokes. Determine how much space you want between the first row of the lower weaving section and the bottom of the rim hoop. For my sample, I used a roll of masking tape as my guide to mark the top of the first row.

TECHNIQUES

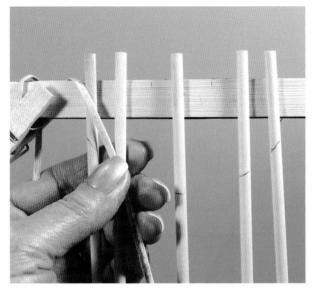

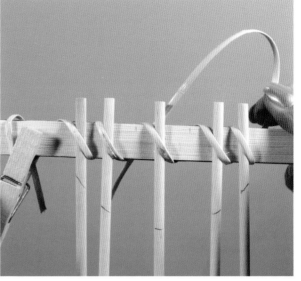

2 Clamp one end of the reed to the back of the left side rim hoop, leaving a 4"–6" (10–15cm) tail that you can tuck into the weaving pattern after the lashing is done. (In this photo, I wrapped the tail around and clamped it too.) Bring the reed over the top of the rim and across the first spoke diagonally.

3 Bring the reed up vertically on the back side between the first and second spokes. This places the reed into position to work the next diagonal spoke crossing. Work the reed in this manner until all of the spokes have been crossed diagonally. End with the reed on the back of the rim on the right side.

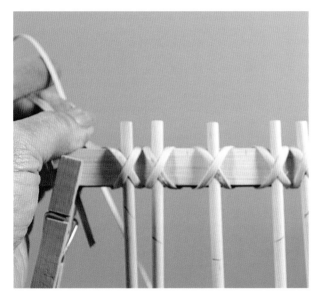

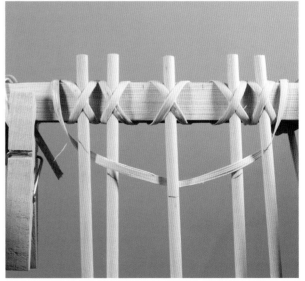

4 Work the lashing pattern in reverse to create the second cross of the X pattern. End with the reed in the original starting position.

5 Work the first row of the lower weaving section by bringing the reed down over the left side rim hoop, giving the reed a quarter twist, and then weaving it through the spokes in an over one under one pattern, as in the previous two ears (pages 65 and 67). At the end of the spokes, give the reed a quarter twist and fold it up over the right side rim hoop.

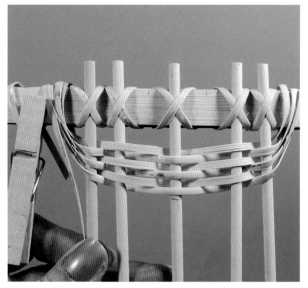

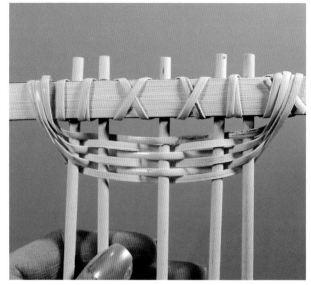

6 Repeat in the reverse direction, as in the previous two ears. Make sure you are maintaining that large air space between the rim hoop and the first row of weaving, if that's your desired effect.

7 Complete this ear by securing the ends of the reed under several loops on the inside of the basket.

WHEEL

The wheel ear allows you to place spokes over the rim hoop as well as under it. This ear is worked using one weaver folded in half, working both ends at the same time in a twining pattern in a counterclockwise direction. This sample is worked over two ½" (1.3cm) hoops, using ¼" flat reed as the weaver.

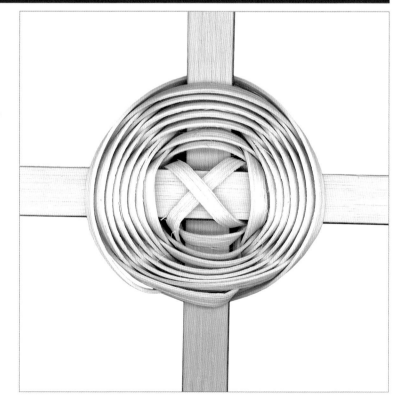

1 Find the center point of the reed, fold it in half, and place the fold over the left side rim hoop. Holding the back reed in place on the back of the rim hoop, bring the front reed over the intersection diagonally. Fold this reed up behind the right side rim hoop so that it ends up in the upper right. Check the photo to make sure everything is placed correctly. From now on, the held side (to the left) will be called the first reed and the wrapped side (to the right) will be called the second reed.

2 Fold the first reed horizontally over the bottom handle hoop.

3 Bring the first reed up behind the right side rim hoop just like you did with the second reed in step 1. Both reeds are now to the upper right of the hoop intersection. The second reed is now on the left and the first reed is now on the right.

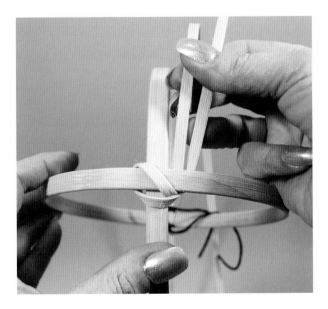

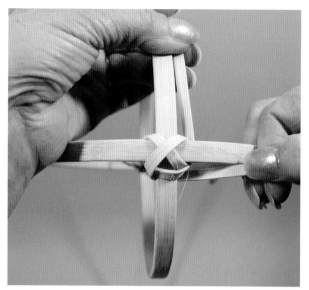

4 Bring the second reed diagonally across the intersection, down to the lower left. Now fold it behind the bottom handle hoop toward the lower right. This means the first reed is above the rim hoop and the second reed is below the rim hoop; both are to the right side of the basket. You have completed the central X pattern and set up the two weavers for the twining pattern.

5 Bring the second reed (the lower reed) up over the right side of the rim hoop. You will now have one reed behind the rim and one in front of the rim.

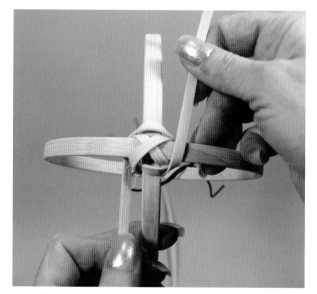

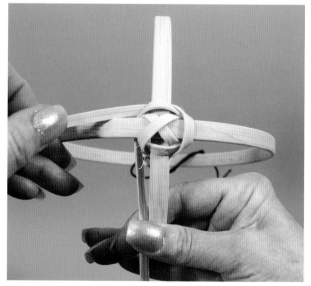

6 Bring the first reed (the one to the back) horizontally over the top handle hoop. Fold this same reed vertically back behind the left side of the rim handle to the lower left.

7 Bring the second reed horizontally under the top handle hoop. You now have one reed in the top left and one in the lower left.

8 Continue weaving the two reeds in this way, working the first reed first, followed by the back reed, and working each reed in the over one under one pattern.

9 Work the wheel pattern until you have woven it to your desired size. Secure the ends of the reeds by tucking them under several loops in the inside of the basket. Clip the excess.

GOD'S EYE/HALF GOD'S EYE COMBINATION

This combination locks the two hoops together with a small God's Eye ear and then creates space for the spokes by working the same weaver into a half God's Eye. See page 53 for the God's Eye instructions and page 62 for the half God's Eye instructions.

1 Begin by working a three-row God's Eye ear over the intersection of the two hoops. End the God's Eye with your reed folded back behind the left rim hoop, leading down.

2 Begin a half God's Eye weave by giving the reed a quarter twist and bringing it horizontally across the bottom handle hoop. Give it another quarter twist and bring it up behind the right rim hoop, then back down over the front, leading down.

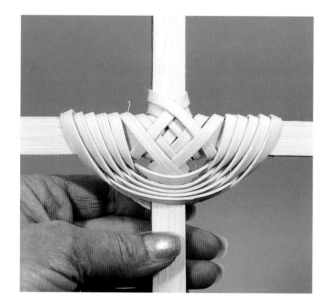

3 Work five rows of the half God's Eye. Tuck and secure the end of the reed and clip off any excess.

DOUBLE BOW/HALF GOD'S EYE COMBINATION

A double bow locks the hoops of the handle and rim together. The extra weaver is then worked in a half God's Eye to accept the spokes. The bow tail of the double bow shows below the half God's Eye's last row of weaving. See page 50 for the double bow instructions and page 62 for the half God's Eye instructions.

1 Work a double bow using ¼" flat reed. This combination also works well using 2.5mm or 3mm cane. Bring the reed vertically up over the right rim hoop and then vertically down on the back side.

2 Continue from this position to create the half God's Eye weaving pattern.

3 Secure the excess weaver in the back of the half God's Eye ear and clip. Clip the excess reed that creates the double bow tail about ½" (1.3cm) below the knot.

REED SPINE LASHING

In place of a handle hoop, you can use a large flat, oval, or half-round reed to create the spine of your basket instead of using thinner round spokes. This provides an extra-strong spine for a basket that will not have a handle.

TECHNIQUES

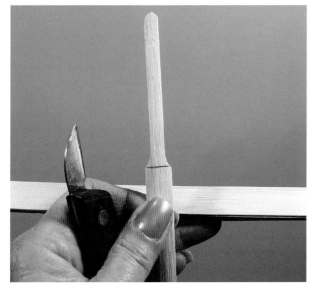

1 Measure a length of ½" half-round reed to the size that you want your basket's spine to be. To this measurement, add 6" (15cm). Cut and soak the reed in warm water. Using a craft knife, trim 3" (7.5cm) of each end to half of its original width. Round over both ends. This will be your new spoke to act as the spine.

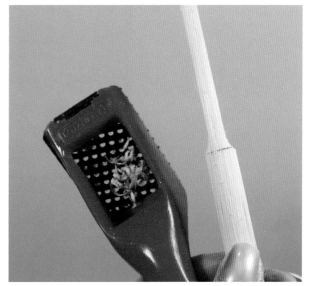

2 With a reed shaver or 220-grit sandpaper, smooth the sides of the spoke where you trimmed them.

3 Fold one trimmed end of the spoke over the rim hoop, with the trimmed side to the back side (inside) of the hoop.

4 The trimmed end of the spoke should extend well below the rim hoop, as shown here on the back side (inside).

5 With ¼" flat reed or, as in this sample, 3mm cane, create a single or double X ear (see page 47) to bind the hoop and spoke together.

6 Continue into a half God's Eye weaving pattern just as you went from a double bow to a half God's Eye on page 77, working each new row over the trimmed end of the back of the spoke with each pass behind the spoke.

7 Secure the end of the reed in the back of the half God's Eye and clip. The finished ear combination creates a strong connection between the spine and the rim hoop that has a low profile along the top edge of the rim hoop.

TECHNIQUES

Branches, antlers, thick grapevine, and even fence wire can become the handle of your basket using this simple lashing technique.

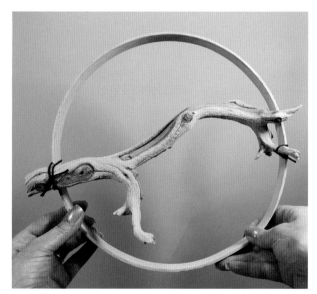

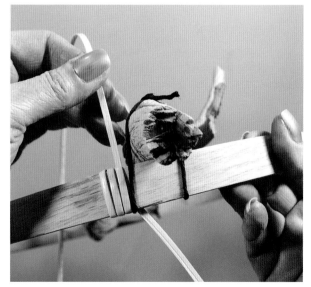

1 Chose an item for your handle that extends 2"–2½" (5–6.3cm) beyond your rim hoop to provide enough space to work the lashing. Using twine, tie the handle into position with a simple square knot wherever the handle crosses the hoop. This holds the handle in place as you work each lashing area with reed.

2 Cane, as is used in this sample, ¼" flat reed, and #2 round reed work well for lashed handles. Hold your reed on the inside of the rim hoop with the end next to the handle. Wrap the rim hoop three to four times with the reed, wrapping over the end of the reed to secure it.

3 Wrap the reed over the handle, bringing the reed down on the other side of the handle to the inside of the rim hoop. Wrap the reed under the rim hoop, then back up over the handle, returning it on the other side to the outside of the rim hoop.

4 Repeat the lashing pattern several times. In this photo, the lashing has been repeated once. When you are satisfied with the lashing, end with the reed on the right side of the handle (the opposite side from the tail end).

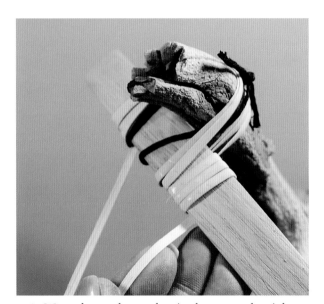

5 Wrap the reed over the rim hoop on the right side three or four times, like you did when you started the lashing in step 2. Secure the end of the reed in the loops on the inside of the hoop and cut the excess.

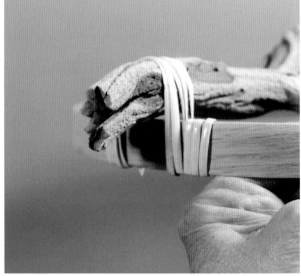

6 Cut and remove the twine you used to secure the handle at the start. The completed lashing firmly holds the handle to the basket. However, it does not create a space to secure your spokes. At this point, you can work a half God's Eye, working the weaver over the beginning and ending loops of the lashing, or you can add a reed spine (see page 78) by feeding the spoke under the handle to fold it over the rim hoop.

Making a Wrapped Handle

After or sometimes before you bind the hoops with an ear, you can add a decorative wrapping to either or both the handle hoop and rim hoop. Wrappings are often worked using ¼" flat reed, cane, or dyed raffia strands. There are many excellent examples on the Internet of wrapped handle patterns used in reed basketry that can easily become part of your rib baskets.

In this basket, the handle is wrapped using 3mm cane and ¼" walnut-dyed flat reed.

1 For this sample, first work a braided God's Eye ear using an extra-long 3mm cane to secure the handle and rim hoop. With the extra cane, work a five-row half God's Eye, which will be used to secure the spokes. Tuck the end of the cane under several loops on the inside of the basket and clip the excess.

2 Cut a length of ¼" walnut-dyed flat reed several inches (7–8cm) longer than the length of the handle hoop you are decorating. Soak the reed for a few minutes, then tuck one end of the reed behind the top of the braided God's Eye, into the space between the two hoops.

3 Tuck one end of a long length of 3mm cane into the same space into which you tucked the walnut-dyed flat reed, behind it. Wrap the 3mm cane around the handle twice, covering the walnut-dyed flat reed.

4 Lift the walnut-dyed flat reed slightly, then wrap the 3mm cane twice around the handle but this time underneath the flat reed.

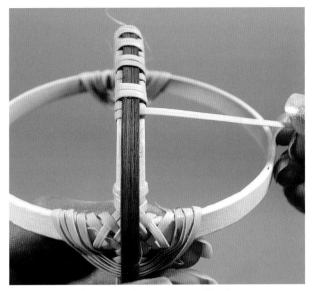

5 Repeat the wrapping pattern of twice over twice under until you are about 2" (5cm) from the braided God's Eye on the opposite side of the basket handle.

6 Clip the excess walnut-dyed flat reed, leaving about ½" to 1" (1.3 to 2.5cm) of reed that can be tucked behind the braided God's Eye. The length of the tucking reed often depends on the width of the rim hoop that you are using. Wider hoops can accept longer lengths, which secure the decorative reed more fully.

7 Continue wrapping the handle with the cane in the established wrapping pattern until you reach the inside top of the braided God's Eye. Tuck the end of the cane through several inner loops of the God's Eye and clip the excess reed.

Spokes

Spokes are the skeleton of the basket over which the weavers are worked. The dimension, length, and placement of the spokes in the ear pattern determine the shape of the walls of your rib basket. Spokes can be made using large round reed (#6–#8), small round reed (#3–#5), half-round or half-oval reed (½" or wider), and wide flat reed (½" or wider). The size and shape of the spoke determines the rollover size of the weavers—that is, how the weavers are broken up into large or small chunks as they are woven. Wide, flat spokes make long rolls. Large, round reed spokes create deep rolls, while small, round reed spokes create tightly packed, low rolls in the weavers.

The spokes form the skeleton of the basket, alongside the hoops.

½" flat reed spokes

#5 round reed spokes

#3 round reed spokes

SPOKE MEASUREMENTS

Throughout the step-by-step basket instructions in chapters 3 and 4, you will find the measurements for the spoke lengths, the type of reed, and the size of reed. These measurements are guidelines only. The actual measurements that you need for the profile of your rib basket can change depending on how tightly you have woven the area into which each spoke will be set. Loose weaving will allow the spoke to be inserted deeply into the space, while tight weaving may only allow the spoke to be inserted under two or three rows of weaving. The length of the taper on the end of the spoke can also affect how deeply the spoke can be inserted. Long tapers of 1" (2.5cm) or more can fit between more woven rows than a short taper of ½" (1.3cm) or less. In general, I cut my spokes slightly longer than the measurement for the area in which it will be inserted. I can then test the fit and recut one end to create a perfect fit. Remember, you can always trim shorter, but you can't untrim!

The pattern of the ear determines where you can anchor the first spokes in your basket. In this sample, the first spokes on each side are inserted into the half God's Eye weave. The top spoke is worked into the top loop of the weave; the second (center) spoke is placed in the intersection of the weave by creating a hole with an awl; and the third is placed in the bottom loop of the weave.

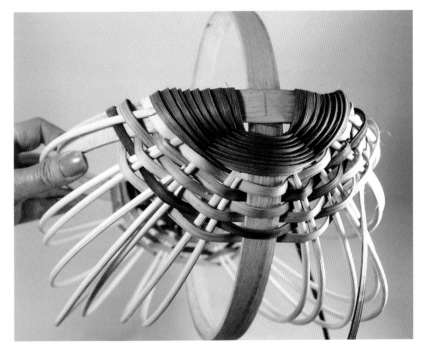

As you work the side walls, you will often need to add new spokes. For this basket, you can see the second round of spokes anchored into the over one under one flat-reed weaving.

Melon Baskets

Using spokes that all have the same length as the lower half of the handle hoop (the part of that hoop that forms the spine) makes your basket into a half-sphere shape, called a melon basket. These spokes are spaced evenly, with an equal distance between each spoke.

Fanny Baskets

Fanny baskets use graduated lengths of spokes that create the two sides of the basket profile. Near the rim hoop, the spokes begin at the same size as the rim hoop. As the spokes near the four and eight o'clock positions, they reach their longest lengths, which pushes the basket wall outward into a low half-oval shape. The spokes nearest the spine shorten to eventually match the spine length.

Hip Baskets

Hip baskets follow the same pattern as fanny baskets but with exaggerated length changes in the spokes to create a very deep, angular division at the spine. The dramatic V-shaped bottom of this style of basket means that a person can place the basket against his or her hip, hold the handle in the crook of the elbow, and have both hands free to work.

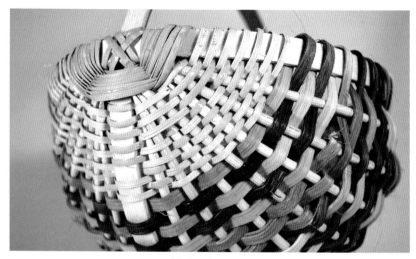

Melon basket

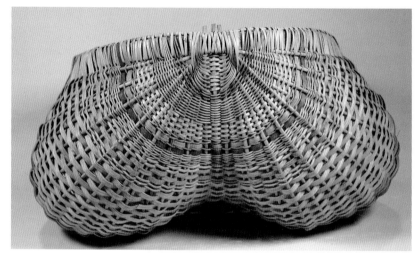

Fanny basket

Hip basket

SPOKE PLACEMENT

Ear patterns create either a large woven area on either side of the spine below the rim hoop, which holds the spokes in place by pressure (as in the God's Eye) or loops created by the weaving pattern into which you can directly insert the spokes (as in the half God's Eye and wheel). The three most common weaving patterns for spoke placement are found with the God's Eye, the half God's Eye, and the wheel ears.

God's Eye Spoke Placement

1 Measure your first spokes so that the point of each spoke reaches the intersection of the two hoops along the desired axis for the spoke. This means that you should hold the spoke where you plan to place it (near the rim, at a 45-degree angle to the rim, etc.). The easiest method for accurate measurement for a melon basket—a round basket in which all of the spokes are basically the same length—is to lay the spoke against one side of the rim hoop and mark it where it touches the center point of each ear. Using a bench knife or craft knife, cut the spoke at the pencil mark.

2 With a knife, sharpen the ends of the spoke to long, tapered points. These long points will be inserted into the space between the weavers of the ear and the hoop intersection itself (see step 3). The more you taper your spokes for this first set, the more space you will have to insert spokes in general, as the tapering will thin out the amount of space taken up in the tight corner.

3 Make sure you have soaked the spokes in warm water for a few moments before inserting them into the basket; this will ensure they are flexible enough to gently bend into the semicircular shape. Place the center spoke first.

4 Add the spokes above and below the center spoke.

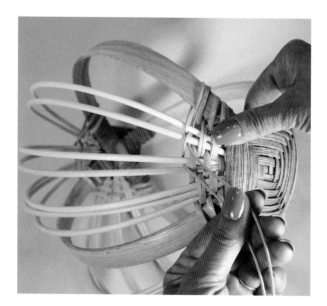

5 Several rows of weaving are worked to secure this first set of spokes. Any weaving pattern can be used. In this sample, the over one under one pattern has been worked using 3mm cane over #3 round reed spokes. A new set of spokes is added when the weave spacing between spokes becomes excessively wide. For tight baskets, this can be a 1" (2.5cm) or smaller space, and for more open woven baskets, new spokes may be needed when you exceed the 1" (2.5cm) measurement. In this sample, one spoke was added alongside the top and middle initial spokes, and two spokes were added alongside the bottom initial spoke.

Half God's Eye Spoke Placement

1 The quarter twist that is worked with the weaver of the half God's Eye ear keeps the weaver tight to the corner intersection of the hoops. It also creates a teardrop-shaped opening between the rows of weaving in which the spokes closest to the rim and spine can be placed.

2 To add a center spoke in a half God's Eye ear, use an awl to split the reeds where they overlap at the center of each side of the ear.

3 Cut the ends of this center spoke into long, tapered points, then insert those points into the awl holes you made on each side.

Wheel-Ear Spoke Placement

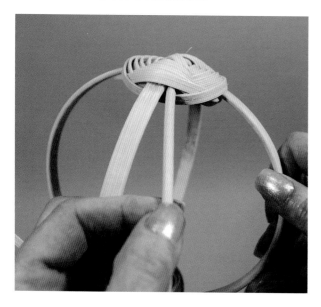

1 The wheel, like the half God's Eye, creates loops near the hoops that are used for spoke placement. Measure and cut your spokes. Cut both ends of the spoke into long, tapered points. Insert the spokes into the wheel loops.

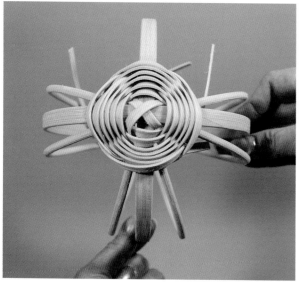

2 Because a wheel ear is worked around all four hoop segments, you can place spokes above the rim hoop and very close to the upper handle hoop. You can also split the overlap area of the wheel weavers with an awl to place a center spoke (as done in the half God's Eye placement). I did not add center spokes to this sample.

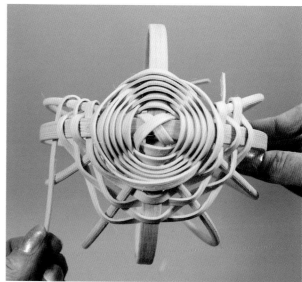

3 Wrap the weavers around the spokes above the rim for each row when you incorporate weavers above the rim hoop.

TECHNIQUES

ADDING DECORATIVE SPOKES

While most spokes you will use in your rib basketry are necessary and contribute to the structural skeleton of the basket, some spokes serve primarily to allow you to add additional decorative weaving. Here are some examples.

In this sample, two ¼" flat spokes were added over the rim hoop to allow the weavers to be worked in an over one under one pattern. Another added spoke, reaching from the hoop intersection to above the rim hoop, is also used for decorative weaving.

The three large central spokes forming the spine for this basket are anchored to the rim hoop using a variation of the three-spoke lashing with X pattern ear. The smaller side spokes are inserted into the handmade round reed handles. This drops the weaving for both sets of spokes well down from the rim.

By adding additional central spokes to a handle hoop basket, you can push the diagonally placed spokes into the side area and away from the handle area. This design uses a bow knot ear to bind the hoops and a three-spoke lashing with X pattern ear for the six central spokes—three on each side of the handle hoop.

Weaving Patterns

Almost all weaving patterns that are used in any style of basketry can be used in your rib baskets. In this section, we'll take a look at the most common weaving patterns and how they can be tweaked to create different variations. Before we get into it, though, it's important to understand the difference between **rolled rows** and **individual rows**. No matter which weaving pattern you choose, your weavers can be worked in two ways in relation to how they connect with the rim: as rolled rows or individual rows.

Rolled rows begin by securing the weaver to the rim, then weaving for one row. When you reach the rim of the opposite side of the basket, the weaver is "rolled" (wrapped or folded) over the rim as if it were simply another spoke and then continued in the weaving pattern back toward the starting point. You can do this for as long as your weaver will allow, going back and forth from side to side without ever

tying a new knot or using a new weaver. Because rolled rows allow you to work very long weavers, your basket's body tends to be stronger and more durable. However, rolling does tilt flat reeds along the rim.

The first fourteen rows of this melon basket (shown at top right) are worked using binding cane in rolled rows. The rolling reveals the back side (beige side) of the caning.

Individual rows (such as the final row in the photo at bottom right) are worked by securing the weaver to the rim, weaving across the spokes, and cutting and securing the weaver on the rim on the opposite side. Individual rows allow a flat reed weaver to lie fully flat against the rim. However, individual rows also create long, exposed, and not tightly secured weaver areas inside the basket. You sometimes have to make decisions about trade-offs between aesthetic appeal and functionality.

Most of these rows of weaving are rolled, but the green and tan raffia and green yarn are all individual rows.

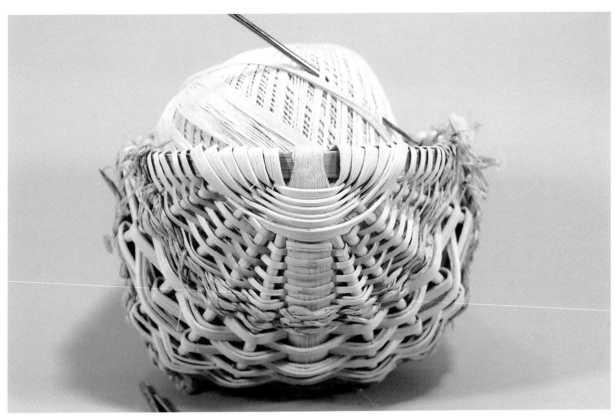

You can see the slight tilting of the rolled rows along the rim in this basket.

The final row here is an individual row.

Weaving Patterns ■ 95

OVER ONE UNDER ONE (O1U1)

This pattern is so common (and is such a mouthful) that it deserves an abbreviation: O1U1. We will use this abbreviation in the rest of the book from this point onward. Work the weaver over one spoke and then under the next spoke. When you roll the row (working rolled rows) or start a new individual row, alternate the weaving pattern by working an "over" on the spoke that holds the "under" of the previous row.

The pattern is started with a 3"–4" (7.6–10cm) tail extending above the rim hoop. That tail is then folded and woven under the main weaver for two to three spokes. This makes a loop that covers the rim and secures the reed in place.

This ¼" mahogany-dyed flat reed is being worked in an O1U1 pattern to add a colored accent row to the basket.

Worked in ¼" flat reed, the O1U1 weaving pattern is the most commonly used pattern in any style of basket construction.

The top row of this sample is worked in #1 round reed, which creates a tightly packed wall. The bottom row of the sample is worked using two #1 round reeds together as if they were one weaver. This technique is called paired weavers or pairing.

Worked using 2.5mm cane, this weave shows off both the top, shiny side of the cane in one row and then the dull, white side in the next. This is easily achieved by making rolled rows (though you could also achieve it by making individual rows).

Double Lemon-Wedge Short Rows

Double lemon-wedge short rows are essentially two separate small lemon wedges, one on each side of the spine, worked separately. In the long, oval split bottom egg basket shown, because the central spokes divide the basket at the spine, each side becomes a separate area that needs short row compensation. You can see the two separate short row areas that were worked just below the last grouping of round reed arrow twine.

Double lemon wedges are more often needed in long, oval baskets where several smaller areas of compensation are used instead of one extremely large (thick) area of short rows. Short rows naturally weaken the basket in that area because the weavers are not wrapped over the rim hoops, so by using multiple lemon-wedge areas, you reduce the stress on the short row weavers.

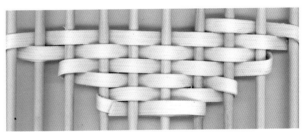

To make this kind of short row, decrease on both sides as you progress.

Saddlebag Short Rows

Saddlebag short rows are essentially two separate small lemon wedges, one on each side of the spine, but connected with just two or three rows of the weaving. Any split bottom basket, like hip baskets and fanny baskets, will need some kind of lemon-wedge short row area on both sides of the spine, and this can be either continuous (as in the lemon wedge), connected (as in the saddlebag), or completely separate (as in the double lemon wedge).

Baskets that are taller than they are wide tend to use the saddlebag short row technique. Here, you are compensating for both the oval shape of the general basket as well as the added depth of the basket sides as they near the spine.

DEALING WITH MULTIPLE SHORT ROW AREAS

Working larger baskets with small-width weavers, like the one shown, gives you plenty of space to use multiple short row areas and to gradually distribute those areas instead of concentrating your compensation into one single large section of the basket walls. Follow along with this basket to see how this can be done.

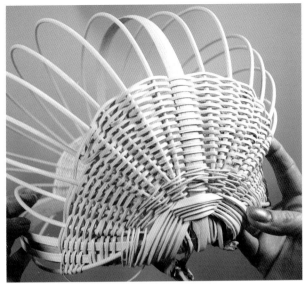

1 The first section of short rows for this design was worked as a lemon wedge. It is quite a small section at the bottom of the weaving completed to this point, culminating on the fifth spoke from the spine. The end of the section is demarcated with a full row of flat reed worked rim to rim.

2 The second short row area was worked directly against the first, using round reed in the arrow twine pattern. The end of the section is demarcated with a full row of ⅜" flat reed worked from rim to rim (visible in the following photo).

3 Because the spokes for the lower section of this basket are far longer than half of the rim size, a third section of short row work was added. The first weave of this short row area is round reed arrow twining, followed by an O1U1 weaving pattern using 2.5mm cane.

CHAPTER 3
STEP-BY-STEP BASKETS

Half God's Eye Hip Basket

This is a great first project for beginners to learn how to apply many of the basic concepts taught in this book. It goes into detail at every step and covers a lot of different techniques. The double X ear low hip basket uses three sets of spokes both to create the gentle upward curve of the bottom area of the basket and to ensure close weaving of the reed for hard daily use. Short row compensation is worked in four different areas along the side walls. These small areas gently transition the half-circle curve of the weaving near the ears into the almost right-angled weaving along the center panel.

SUPPLIES

- Two 10" diameter x ½" width (25.5 x 1.3cm) round oak hoops
- 1 yard (1m) of twine
- Measuring tape
- Pencil
- Scissors or reed cutters
- Craft knife
- Flat packing tool
- Soaking pan and warm water
- 220-grit sandpaper
- Nylon-grip flat-nosed pliers
- Spray-on polyurethane sealer

SPOKES AND WEAVERS

- ⅝" natural flat reed (double X ear)
- ¼" natural flat reed (Weave 1)
- ¼" space-dyed walnut flat reed (Weave 7, 9)
- ¼" natural flat oval reed (Weave 2, 10, 11, 12, 13)
- 3mm cane (Weave 6, 8)
- #5 natural round reed (Spoke Set 1, 2, 3)
- #2 oak-dyed round reed (Weave 3, 5)
- Loose raffia strands (Weave 4)

SPOKE CUTTING

- Spoke Sets 1, 2, and 3: cut 38 total from #5 round reed
  Lengths as described in steps 12, 20, and 44

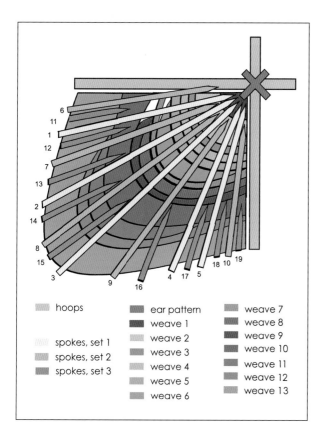

Legend:
- hoops
- spokes, set 1
- spokes, set 2
- spokes, set 3
- ear pattern
- weave 1
- weave 2
- weave 3
- weave 4
- weave 5
- weave 6
- weave 7
- weave 8
- weave 9
- weave 10
- weave 11
- weave 12
- weave 13

A Note about the Diagrams

For all of the basket project diagrams in this book, the spokes are numbered by sets—one group of spokes that are added to the basket frame at one time. For example, this particular design uses three sets of spokes. The first set is inserted into Weave 1, the half God's Eye pattern; the second is inserted into Weave 2, made of ¼" flat oval reed in an O1U1 pattern; and the third is inserted into Weave 10, made of ¼" flat oval reed in an O1U1 pattern. Within a spoke set, the spokes are numbered from top to bottom—closest (almost parallel) to the rim down to closest (almost parallel) to the spine. However, the numbering of the spokes within a set does not necessarily correlate to the order in which the spokes are inserted into the basket frame.

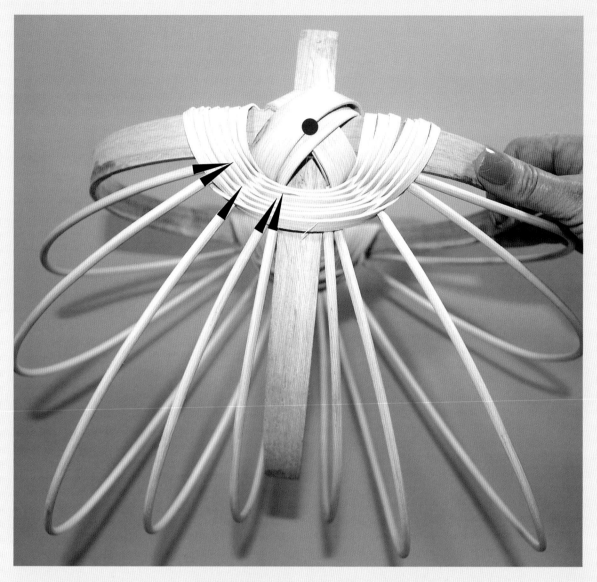

Cutting the Spokes for Spoke Set 1

In this project, the first set of spokes is inserted into the half God's Eye in the loops and in the crossover area created from the weaving. Spokes seldom reach as deeply into an eye pattern as the first row of weaving in the eye. You may only be able to insert a spoke halfway or less into this area.

The measurement for each spoke is not worked from the center of the hoop intersection (shown as a red dot) but rather from where you estimate that the tip of that spoke will penetrate the weaving that will support it. For example, for the top spoke shown here, the measurement from the center of the hoop intersection (red dot) to the center of the hoop intersection on the opposite side of the basket is 19" (48cm), but the given measurement to follow (and the final measurement for the spoke itself) is only 15½" (39cm) (to the black point).

How deeply any particular spoke can be set can be unpredictable. Cut new spokes slightly longer than the project measurements, insert them into place, and then trim as needed.

Spoke Set 1

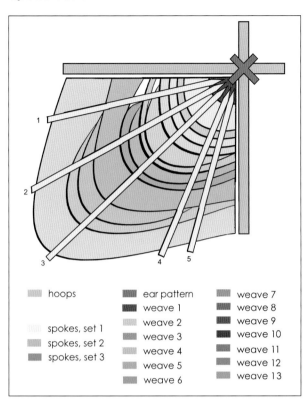

hoops

spokes, set 1
spokes, set 2
spokes, set 3

ear pattern
weave 1
weave 2
weave 3
weave 4
weave 5
weave 6

weave 7
weave 8
weave 9
weave 10
weave 11
weave 12
weave 13

12 Here is a simplified version of the full diagram so you can see only the spokes to be added in Spoke Set 1. Cut two of each spoke in Spoke Set 1 from #5 round reed. Here are the spoke measurements:
#1: 15½" (39.4cm)
#2: 19" (48.3cm)
#3: 22½" (57.2cm)
#4: 20½" (52.1cm)
#5: 18½" (47cm)

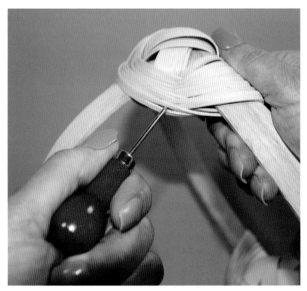

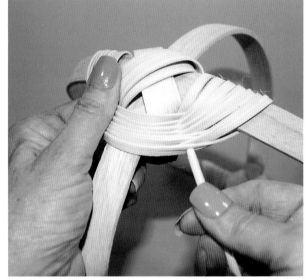

13 The first spoke to be inserted is spoke #3. Using an awl, pierce the crossover area of the half God's Eye that is between the rim and spine on both sides of the basket. This creates a hole in which the spoke can be set.

14 Sharpen both ends of spoke #3 to a point that is ½" (1.3cm) long. Insert the point into the awl hole. Push the spoke as deeply as you can into the hole. Insert the other end of the spoke into the corresponding awl hole on the far end of the basket. Repeat with the second spoke #3 on the other side of the basket.

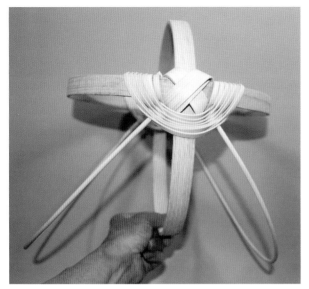

15 Position these spokes at a 45-degree angle between the rim hoop and the spine. These spokes are the longest spokes in the basket and define the outer edge of the basket wall's curve.

16 Insert spoke #2 into the opening in the half God's Eye directly under the rim. Bring the other end of the spoke all the way to the far end of the basket. Hold the spoke over the half God's Eye and adjust its length until you find the outer point of the curve that you want for your basket shape. Mark with your thumb where the spoke will tuck into the half God's Eye. Cut the spoke at this point, sharpen, and insert it into the eye. Repeat with the second spoke #2 on the other side of the basket.

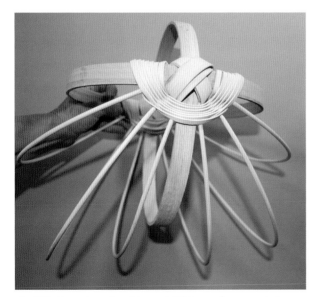

17 Insert spoke #4 next. This spoke goes into the half God's Eye opening next to the spine. Do this for both sides of the basket.

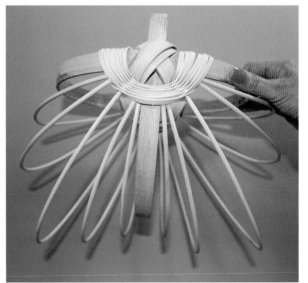

18 Place spoke #1 above spoke #2, into the same half God's Eye opening as spoke #2. Place spoke #5 below spoke #4 so that it lies closest to the spine. It is inserted into the same half God's Eye opening as spoke #4. You now have five spokes on each side of your basket frame.

Weave 2 (¼″ natural flat oval reed)

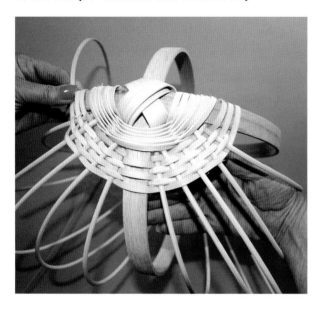

19 With ¼" natural flat oval reed, work 6 rows of O1U1 weaving over the spokes. This creates three loops on each side of the rim hoop. Secure the flat oval reed on the inside of the basket by weaving it back over itself on the last row of weaving for two to three spokes.

Spoke Set 2

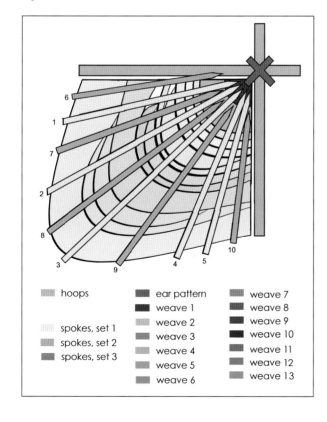

hoops	ear pattern	weave 7
	weave 1	weave 8
spokes, set 1	weave 2	weave 9
spokes, set 2	weave 3	weave 10
spokes, set 3	weave 4	weave 11
	weave 5	weave 12
	weave 6	weave 13

20 Here is a simplified version of the full diagram so you can see the spokes to be added in Spoke Set 2. Cut and sharpen two of each spoke in Spoke Set 2 from #5 round reed. Here are the spoke measurements:
  #6: 13½" (34.3cm)
  #7: 16" (40.6cm)
  #8: 19" (48.3cm)
  #9: 20" (50.8cm)
  #10: 14½" (36.8cm)

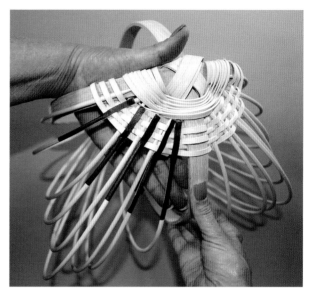

21 The second set of spokes to be added will be set into the O1U1 weaving of the ¼" flat oval reed (Weave 2). Note that the top new spoke is able to reach all the way into the half God's Eye, while the lowest new spoke goes into only 3 or so rows of the flat oval work (Weave 2). (In this photo, spoke #10 has not been added yet, but it is part of Spoke Set 2.)

22 I have marked Spoke Set 1 with blue painter's tape so that you can easily distinguish Set 1 from Set 2. Insert spoke #6 at the midpoint of the space between the rim hoop and spoke #1. Insert spokes #7, #8, and #9 into the same spaces as the Set 1 spokes, placing the new spokes above the original spokes (see the diagram). Insert spoke #10 at the midpoint between spoke #5 and the spine (not shown in this photo).

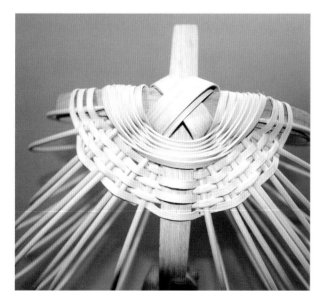

23 You will now have ten working spokes, and the outer curvature of your basket wall should be developing into an elongated half-oval with spoke #1 as the longest point in the curve from the double X ear. (Note: As I was creating this basket, I didn't add spoke #10 until around step 27, so you will not see all ten spokes appearing in the photos until then.)

Weave 3 (#2 oak-dyed round reed)

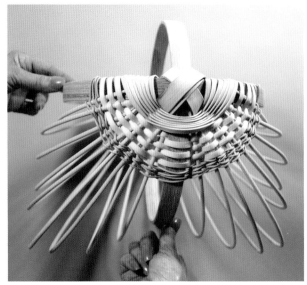

24 Using #2 oak-dyed round reed, work 4 rows of arrow twining. You will have two full arrows in this area of weaving with two to three round reed loops over the rim hoop.

25 Arrow twining not only creates a decorative weave, it also slowly separates the newly inserted spokes (Spoke Set 2) from the original set of spokes (Spoke Set 1).

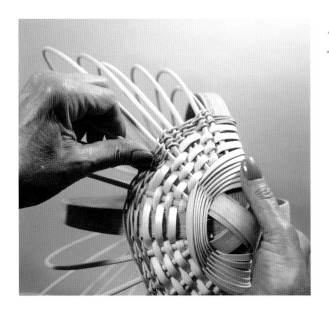

26 Now that the second set of spokes is locked into the basket frame and slightly separated from the original spokes, you can begin adjusting all of the spokes to create a smooth, curved line along the profile of your basket. Gently pull shorter spokes out of the weaving until they align with your curves. Spokes that are too long can be pushed deeper into the weaving. Occasionally, an extra-long spoke will need to be completely removed from the weaving on one side of the basket and the point recut to suit the curvature. The weavers that surround the area of such spokes are stiff and strong enough to retain the channel for the spoke so that it can easily be reinserted once cut.

Weave 4 (loose raffia strands)

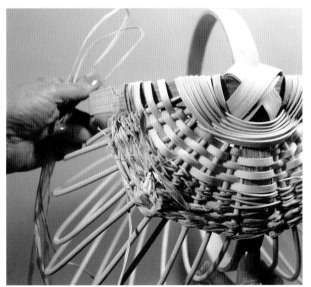

27 Using several strands of loose raffia held together to be worked as one weaver, create 8 rows of twining. Begin and end each row on the top spoke (spoke #6) of the basket frame rather than the rim itself. There will be four raffia loops on this spoke, and the rim hoop will have an unworked space that measures about 1" (2.5cm) wide.

Weave 5 (#2 oak-dyed round reed)

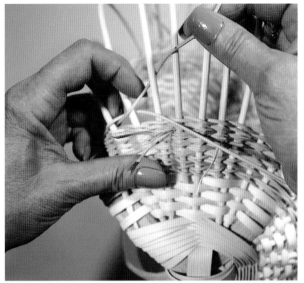

28 Using #2 oak-dyed round reed, work 4 rows of arrow twining. You will have two full arrows in this area of weaving with two to three round reed loops over the rim hoop.

Complete Marking for Short Rows (on page 120) before continuing to step 29.

Weave 6: First Short Row Area (3mm cane)

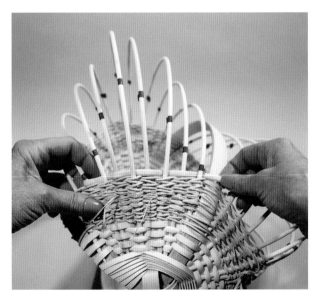

29 With 3mm cane, begin an O1U1 weaving pattern on the third spoke from the rim hoop (spoke #1). Work the weaver to the spoke that lies next to the spine (spoke #10). Turn the weaver around this spoke (don't continue to the spine).

Marking for Short Rows

Because each spoke of this rib basket is a different length at some point in your weaving, you cannot continue with only straight row weaving that goes from one side of the rim to the other.

The weaving that has already been worked now covers approximately one quarter of the spine on each side of the basket. This is an excellent place to begin working areas of short rows (see page 101 for more detail). Each short row helps to fill the excess space on the long spokes.

Here is a technique that you can use to measure and mark the short rows on this project. It is slightly different than the techniques shown on pages 101–105; any of the techniques will work, but this is what I used for this particular basket.

1. With a tape measure, measure the length of unworked space along the spine. This is the distance from the edge of the twining (Weave 5) on one side of the hoop to the edge of the twining on the other side.
2. Make a simple template of lightweight cardboard that is ½" (1.3cm) wide by the length of the unworked hoop measurement. Fold this template in half lengthwise.
3. Measure and mark the center point of each spoke with a pencil. Place the center (the fold) of your template on the center pencil mark of each spoke. Make a pencil mark on both sides of the template on each spoke. This marks the area of each spoke that is the same length as the unworked area of the spine.
4. For extra visual clarity, place a small strip of painter's tape at each of the pencil marks. The space between the last row of twining (Weave 5) and the tape or pencil mark is the area that will need to be worked with short rows to compensate for the changing length of spokes in this basket.

You can work short row compensation either as one large area or by working several small areas of short rows intermixed with normal rim-to-rim weavers. For this basket, we will create two small areas of short rows with a rim-to-rim weaver between each area, followed by a larger short row area near the center of the basket frame.

Spoke Set 3

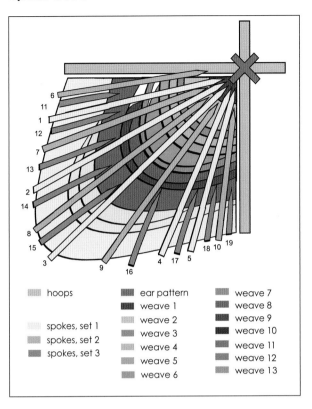

hoops

spokes, set 1
spokes, set 2
spokes, set 3

ear pattern
weave 1
weave 2
weave 3
weave 4
weave 5
weave 6

weave 7
weave 8
weave 9
weave 10
weave 11
weave 12
weave 13

44 Here is a simplified version of the full diagram so you can see the spokes to be added in Spoke Set 3. Cut and sharpen two of each spoke in Spoke Set 3 from #5 round reed. Here are the spoke measurements (but see step 47 before proceeding):

#11: 6" (15.2cm)
#12: 8¼" (21cm)
#13: 8" (20.3cm)
#14: 8½" (21.6cm)
#15: 10" (25.4cm)
#16: 10" (25.4cm)
#17: 9½" (24.1cm)
#18: 8" (20.3cm)
#19: 7" (17.8cm)

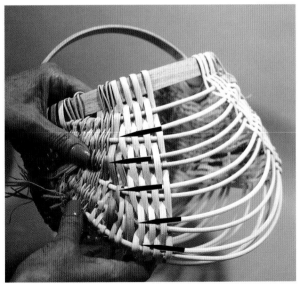

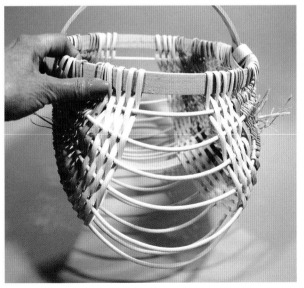

45 The spokes for Spoke Set 3 rest in the O1U1 ¼" flat oval weaving (Weave 10). To achieve the proper curvature of the new spokes, you may find that some of them can be tucked into the weaving as deeply as five rows, while others may only go into three rows.

46 Decorative rib baskets can have large open spaces between the spokes, as shown in this photo. From a side view, the spokes are approximately 1" to 1¼" (2.5 to 3.2cm) apart. Wider weavers, ⅜" or wider, can be used to fill spokes that have a wide spacing.

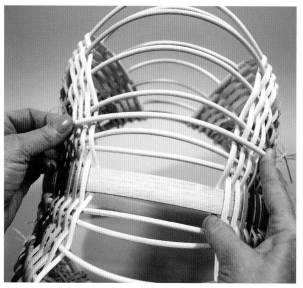

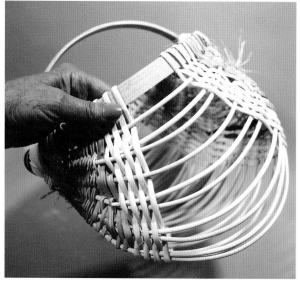

47 Working baskets, though, those that will be under the daily stress of use, need smaller spacing between the spokes to ensure a tight and secure basket wall. For this basket, therefore, I am adding one spoke between each of the existing spokes, starting with the space between spoke #1 and #7. Measure each spoke by laying your #5 round reed over the area to be filled. Allowing this spoke to be inserted under three to four rows of weaving on both sides, mark where you need to cut the reed. Sharpen the ends and insert the new spoke.

48 Spokes #11 through #15 are inserted with the point of the new spoke above the existing spokes. Spokes #16 through #19 are inserted with the point of the new spoke below the existing spokes. See the diagram.

Weave 13 (¼" natural flat oval reed)

49 (Note that this is Weave 13, not 11! We are going out of order. You'll see why later.) Begin working the center panel area of the side walls by placing the lengthwise center of a ¼" natural flat oval reed on the center point of the unworked spine. Work one side of the weaver in an O1U1 pattern down the center line of the basket wall, across the entire basket.

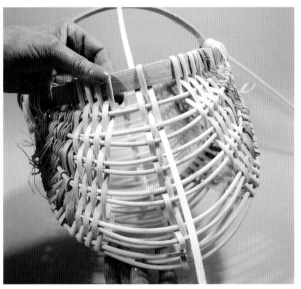

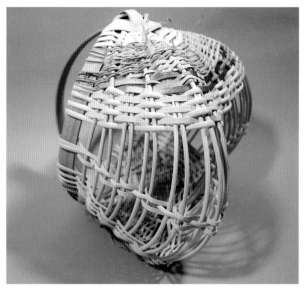

50 Work the remaining side of the weaver along its corresponding side of the center. You will have 3 woven rows at this point.

51 Measure the distances between your newly woven rows and the finished weaving worked previously (Weave 10). Adjust these rows as necessary to ensure that they fall as evenly balanced down the center as possible.

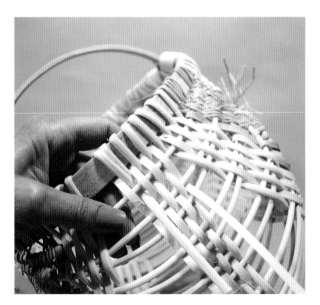

52 Continue working one side of the weaver in the O1U1 pattern for 6 rows. This gives you 1 center row plus 6 new rows on one side of the center. During this stage of the work, I will finish one side of the basket, working the weavers until I have reached the previously woven areas, and then work the second, remaining, side of the basket. You can also work both sides through each of the steps. Either process creates an excellent finished basket.

Weave 12: Short Row (¼" natural flat oval reed)

53 On the eighth row of O1U1 weaving (continuing from step 52), begin working short rows, turning the first short row around on spoke #6. Note in this photo that the center weaving along the rim touched the previous weaving that was worked from the ear area. It was this touch-point that determined when the short row work began.

54 The beginning of my short row work also happened to occur at a place in the weaving where I needed to add a new weaver.

55 Continue working in the O1U1 pattern. When the weaver finds the touch-point between the center panel weaving and the ear weaving, turn the weaver around on that particular spoke.

56 When the weaver finds the touch-point near the spine, turn the weaver around on that spoke.

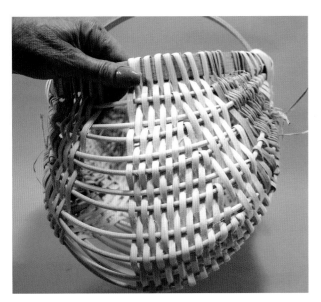

57 Continue working the short rows until all of the open space on the spokes has been worked. Again, do not overly pack this area with weavers. It is easier to add an extra weaver after the basket has dried than to try to force a weaver into the basket wall on the other side of the frame when you mirror your short row turns. When one side of the frame is complete, work the remaining side of the basket. Refer to the number of rows that you needed on the first side and which spokes you turned each row around on to create a mirror image of the weaving.

Weave 11: Filling In after Drying (¼" natural flat oval reed)

58 You will have noticed that a weaving area has been marked as Weave 11 in the diagram, but we have not worked an area of weaving for it. As your basket dries over several days, both the reeds and spokes will shrink slightly. That can cause the weaving to become loose or create small open spaces between rows. With your fingers, gently begin to pack the weavers tightly against each other. Push the rows just enough so that the weavers come into contact with each other but are not so tight that they begin to overlap other weavers. Packing like this can open a space in the wall of your basket that will require one or two new weavers to be inserted.

I prefer to pack the center panel of weaving (Weaves 12 and 13) toward the side center. This maintains and protects the O1U1 weaving pattern that you have worked so carefully to create through this area. I pack the curved area of weaving (Weaves 10 through 11) toward the ear area. All of this puts the open space created by the packing in the area marked on the diagram as Weave 11. The two or four weavers that may be needed to fill the open space can easily be woven along the short row work done in this area without disturbing the center panel weaving. Remember that you want to add packing weavers in pairs—one on each side of the basket frame. Add these new packing rows with the same weaving reed of one of the adjacent woven areas and work them as individual rows.

God's Eye Melon Basket with Decorative Spoke

This classic melon basket with a God's Eye ear will take you through the steps of creating the God's Eye ear pattern to secure the two hoops, setting your starting spokes, adding new spokes, and working in a decorative spoke. It uses an O1U1 weaving pattern as well as arrow twining to fill the sides.

SUPPLIES

- Two 10" diameter x ¾" width (25.5 x 2cm) oak hoops
- 1 yard (1m) of twine
- Measuring tape
- Pencil
- Scissors or reed cutters
- Craft knife
- Flat packing tool
- Soaking pan and warm water
- 220-grit sandpaper
- Nylon-grip flat-nosed pliers
- Spray-on polyurethane sealer

SPOKES AND WEAVERS

- ¼" light walnut-dyed flat reed (God's Eye ear)
- ¼" dark walnut-dyed flat reed (Weave 3, 4, 5)
- ¼" natural flat reed (Weave 6)
- ¼" oak-dyed flat reed (Weave 7)
- 3mm cane (Weave 1)
- #3 to #5 round reed (Spoke Set 1, 2, and 3)
- #1 to #2 round reed (Weave 2)
- 12" x ⅛" (30 x 0.3cm) bamboo kitchen skewer

SPOKE CUTTING

- Spoke Set 1 and Spoke Set 2: cut 14 total from #3, #4, or #5 round reed
  Lengths as described in step 13
- Spoke Set 3: cut 2 from #3, #4, or #5 round reed
  Lengths as described in step 45

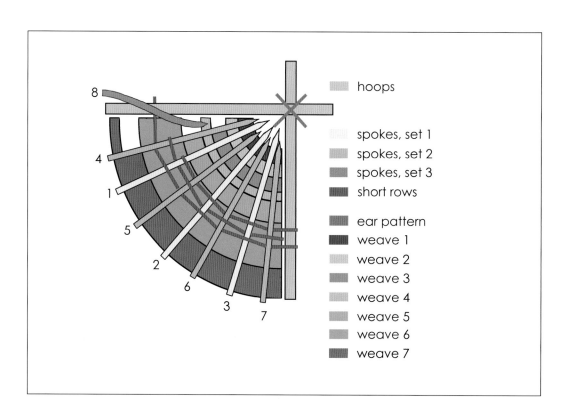

hoops

spokes, set 1
spokes, set 2
spokes, set 3
short rows

ear pattern
weave 1
weave 2
weave 3
weave 4
weave 5
weave 6
weave 7

God's Eye Ear (¼" light walnut-dyed flat reed)

1 Make a pencil mark on one spot on one hoop. Use a measuring tape to determine the circumference of the hoop, divide that number by 2, and use this measurement to make a mark exactly halfway around the hoop, directly opposite the first mark you made. Repeat the entire marking process with the second hoop.

2 Insert the handle hoop inside the rim hoop, matching up the pencil marks. Use twine to temporarily tie the two hoops together where they intersect on both sides. The God's Eye ear will be worked clockwise around the hoop intersection, going from the upper handle hoop, to the right rim hoop, to the spine hoop, and ending with the left rim hoop. (The spine hoop is the lower handle hoop.)

3 Hold the end of a ¼" light walnut-dyed flat reed behind one hoop intersection on a diagonal from the top right to the bottom left.

4 Bring the reed diagonally across the intersection from the bottom left to the upper right.

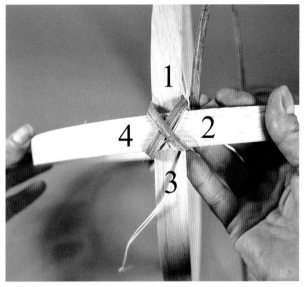

5 Fold the reed back behind the upper handle hoop horizontally from right to left.

6 Bring the reed diagonally across the intersection from the upper left to the lower right. Then fold it up behind the right rim hoop vertically to bring it to the upper right.

7 Bring the reed diagonally across the intersection from the upper right to the lower left. Then fold it back behind the spine horizontally from left to right. Continue by bringing the reed diagonally across the intersection from the lower right to the upper left.

8 Finally, fold the reed vertically down behind the left rim hoop. In this photo, you can see the entire weaving sequence from step 4 to step 9.

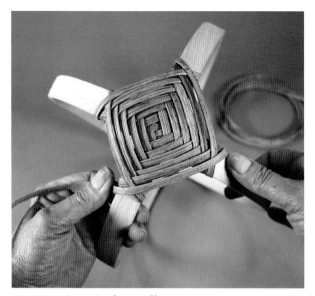

9 Continue in the God's Eye weaving pattern until you have worked 7 full rows. (If you need further help weaving this ear, see the instructions on page 53.) End the weaving when you cross the diagonal to the lower left.

10 Insert the flat packing tool under several loops of the weave on the inside rim of the basket, above the working weaver. In this case, it is on the spine.

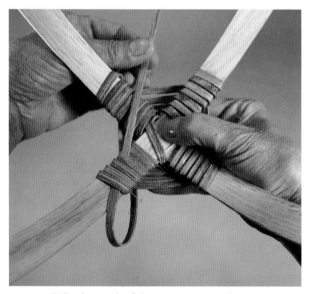

11 Slide the end of the weaver into the space created by the packing tool. Pull the weaver tight so that it is secured under the loops.

12 Cut the excess weaver with a craft knife. Use the knife to cut away the twine that originally held the two hoops together at the intersections. The God's Eye pattern is complete. Repeat all steps to create a second God's Eye on the other hoop intersection.

Spoke Set 1

13 To create medium-sized spokes, use #3, #4, or #5 round reed. Soak one length of round reed in your water pan. Use your hands to pull or work that reed as straight as possible. Place one end of the reed at the center of one God's Eye knot. Bend it along the rim hoop and mark where the reed meets the center of the other God's Eye knot. Cut the reed at this mark, which is about half of the circumference of the rim hoop. Cut thirteen more spokes of the same size, for a total of fourteen. This basket is a fully round melon basket that uses spokes of all the same length.

14 With your craft knife, taper both ends of all of the spokes to narrow points about 1" (2.5cm) long. Sand the tapers lightly with 220-grit sandpaper.

15 Set aside eight spokes for use later; right now, you need six spokes. Insert the first spoke under one side of the God's Eye knot, at the center point of the hoop intersection. Insert the other end of the spoke in the same position on the opposite God's Eye. This is spoke #2.

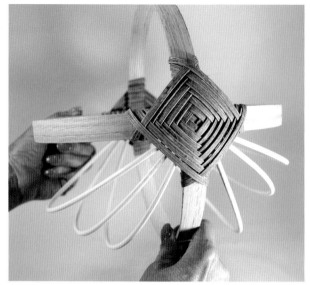

16 Position one spoke above the first, inserting it under the God's Eye in the space between the rim hoop and the first spoke. Secure the other end of the spoke into the other God's Eye in the same position. Repeat to position a third spoke below the first, between the first spoke and the spine. Then repeat on the opposite side of the spine, using the three remaining spokes. These are spokes #1 and #3.

17 Gently move the three spokes on each side to evenly space them. This is your completed first set of spokes.

Weave 1 (3mm cane)

18 Tuck one end of a length of 3mm cane under several loops of the God's Eye weaving on the left side of the rim hoop so that the shiny or finished side of the cane will be visible when the cane is pulled to the front. Bring the cane up over the rim hoop on the left side. Weave it in an O1U1 pattern through the three spokes, spine, remaining three spokes, and right side rim hoop. Count the left side rim hoop as the first "over" weave in the O1U1 pattern.

19 Roll the cane over the right side rim and continue weaving in the O1U1 pattern. On this row, the back side, or dull side, of the cane will be visible.

20 The second row of O1U1 weaving will end with the cane on the inside of the left side rim.

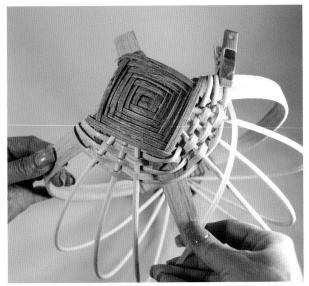

21 Continue the O1U1 pattern for 5 rows total. You will end with the shiny side of the cane passing over the right side rim. You can clamp it as shown.

22 Tuck the end of this weaver under several spokes of the last row. This creates a loop that goes around the rim hoop and first spoke (see top center of photo). Cut the excess cane.

Spoke Set 2

23 Insert four new spokes on each side of the spine, using up the eight spokes you set aside earlier. The first new spoke, spoke #4, goes directly above the top spoke of Spoke Set 1 (spoke #1). The second new spoke, spoke #5, goes directly above the middle spoke of Spoke Set 1 (spoke #2). The final two new spokes, spokes #6 and #7, go directly above and below the bottom spoke of Spoke Set 1 (spoke #3).

Weave 2 (#1 or #2 round reed)

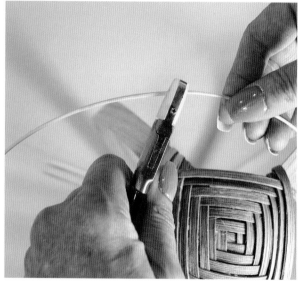

24 Find the center of a piece of #1 or #2 round reed and gently flatten a 3"–4" (7.6–10cm) length by squeezing with nylon-grip flat-nosed pliers. This makes folding the round reed over the rim hoop easier and keeps the reed from splitting.

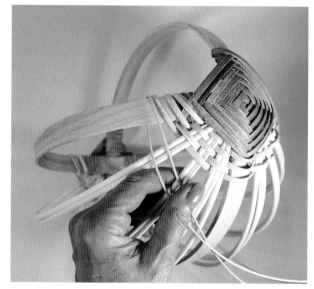

25 Place the crimped center of the reed over the left side rim hoop. This places one side of the reed on the inside of the basket and one on the outside.

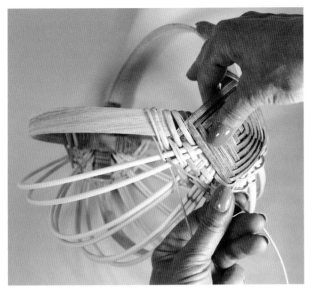

26 Weave the outside reed under the first spoke, which is one of the newly added spokes from Spoke Set 2 (spoke #4). Weave the inside reed over the first spoke. This pulls the new spoke away from the top spoke from Spoke Set 1 (spoke #1).

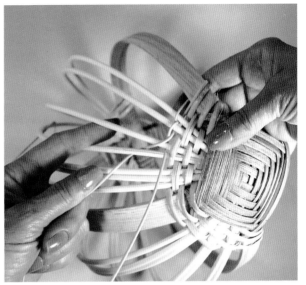

27 Continue weaving in a twining pattern (see page 97). This will become an arrow twining pattern later, but for the first row of any arrow twining pattern, it's just a basic twining pattern.

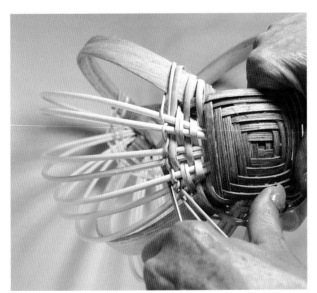

28 As you work the weaver, use an awl or your flat packing tool to tightly pack the new rows of weaving against the previous rows.

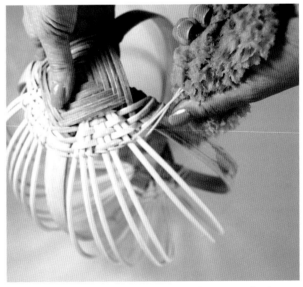

29 Use a damp sea sponge or large synthetic sponge to refresh your weaver with water to keep it supple as you work.

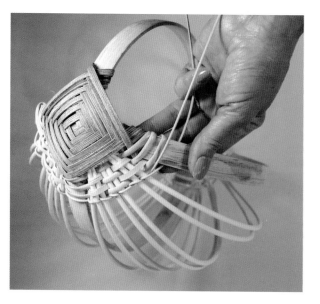

30 Work this twining pattern until you reach the other side of the rim hoop and have opened the spacing between all of the spokes. To create the second row of the arrow twining pattern, and to actually start creating the arrow effect, first finish the first row by placing one reed strand over the rim and one behind the rim.

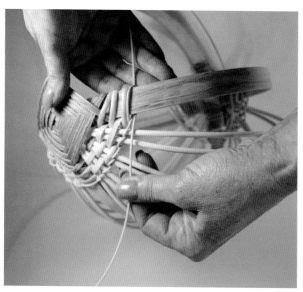

31 Roll the upper strand over the rim, bringing it around to the back.

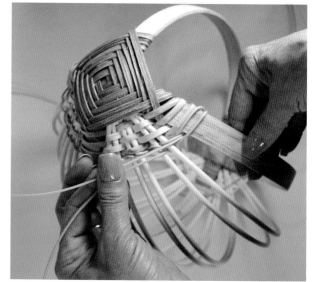

32 Roll the remaining strand over the rim and insert the end next to the reed you just worked. This puts the two working ends side by side, at the back of the rim, with their rollover loop on either side of the working reeds.

Spoke Set 3

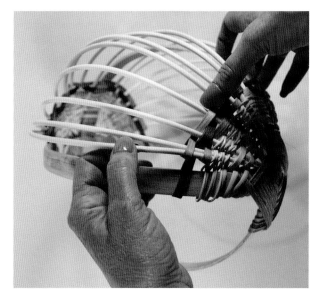

45 Now it's time to add spoke #8, the final spoke. Place a #3 to #5 round reed length against the top spoke and hold the end where it will tuck into the weaving that you have already worked. Hold the reed on the opposite side of the basket and, with your fingers, mark where the reed will tuck into the weave on this side. Now gently slide the reed until it extends about ½" (1.3cm) in front of the top spoke. This makes the new spoke measurement a little longer than the measurement of the current top spoke. Reposition your hand to where the reed will now tuck into the weaving and mark with a pencil. Cut the spoke. Cut a second spoke to the same measurement. (In this photo, the new spoke has already been added per step 46.)

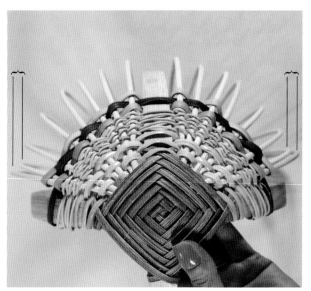

46 Cut both ends of both spokes to a tapered point. Insert the new spokes into the weaving above the top spokes. You can see the slight length difference between the new spoke (spoke #8) and the existing top spoke (spoke #4) in this photo.

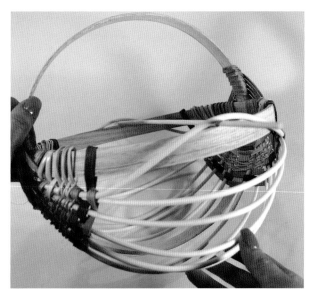

47 Now gently lift the center point of these new spokes above the rim hoop, into position roughly, as shown in the finished project photo. Slide a bamboo skewer under the new spokes, resting the skewer on the top of the rim.

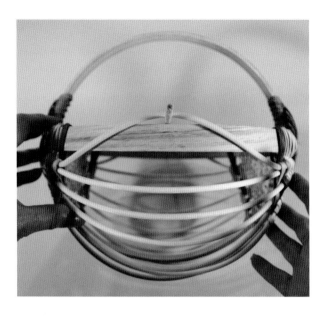

48 Adjust the tucked spoke ends as necessary to bring the new spoke down on top of the skewer. This gives the new spokes a gentle curve that reaches from the main basket wall area to above the rim hoops.

Weave 6 (¼" natural flat reed)

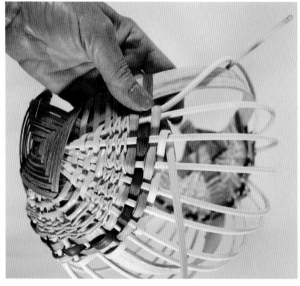

49 Secure a new ¼" natural flat reed weaver on what is now the third spoke from the top on the left side of the basket (spoke #1). (Secure following the technique described in Weave 3.) Work this weaver in an O1U1 pattern for 1 row to reach the opposite side of the basket. Roll the weaver over the third spoke (spoke #1) on that side and work a new row to return to the starting point.

50 When you reach the left side again, this time continue up to the second spoke from the top (spoke #4). Roll the weaver over the second spoke and work a new row to go all the way to the opposite side of the basket again. Then roll the weaver over the second spoke on that side (spoke #4) and work a new row to come back again to the left side. Now, instead of rolling over on the second spoke, bring the weaver all the way up to roll over the rim, skipping the top (decorative) spoke (spoke #8) completely by passing beneath it.

Adding a New Weaver

If at any time you need to seamlessly add a new length of ¼" flat reed to continue the desired pattern, place the end of the new reed under the end of the old weaver, overlapping for several inches. Work the two weavers as if they were one. After working the pair over two to three spokes, drop the old weaver and continue with the new one.

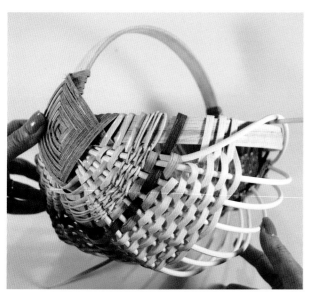

51 Make a total of 8 rows back and forth, always rolling over the rim and skipping the top (decorative) spoke (spoke #8) completely by passing beneath it. At the end, you should have five loops on each side of the rim, and the working end should be on the left side of the basket. (In this photo, not all of the full rows have been completed.)

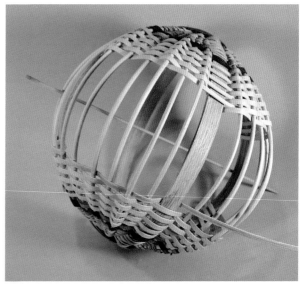

52 Take a few moments and double-check the packing of your weaves at this point in the work. Rewet the weavers if necessary, using a damp sea sponge.

53 Make another row back to the right side of the basket, but this time stop and roll over on the second spoke (spoke #4) instead of the rim. Proceed to create 3 more rows this way, always rolling over the second spoke. At the end, you should finish on the left side of the basket. Important: Instead of securing the working end and cutting off the excess as you normally would, first work in a new ¼" oak-dyed flat reed weaver. (This is what you'll use for Weave 7.) Then secure the working end of the natural reed and cut the excess. When you repeat all steps to create Weave 6 on the other side of the basket, secure the working end of the natural reed and cut off the excess as you normally would—you only need to work Weave 7 from one direction, so you only need to add the oak-dyed reed once.

Weave 7 (¼" oak-dyed flat reed)

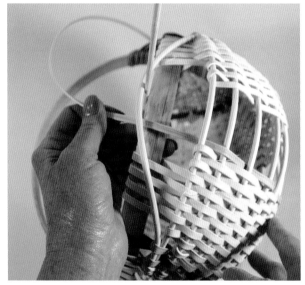

54 Work 1 row of O1U1 with the oak-dyed reed you added in step 53. When you reach the rim hoop on the far side of the basket, bring the weaver over the rim but under the decorative spoke (spoke #8).

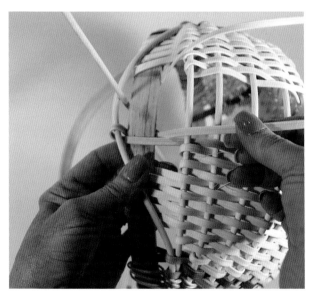

55 Wrap the end of the weaver around the decorative spoke (spoke #8) to create a loop on it. Feed the end of the weaver behind the rim hoop between the decorative spoke and the rim.

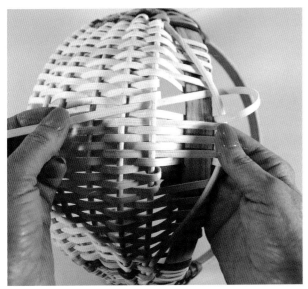

56 Continue working the O1U1 pattern this way, wrapping the weaver around the decorative spoke (spoke #8) each time you reach the rim hoop, until you have filled the remaining space in the basket wall. Be sure to end the last row of weaving so that it fits into the O1U1 pattern of the two adjoining rows (see photo) instead of having two matched rows next to each other. Cut the excess.

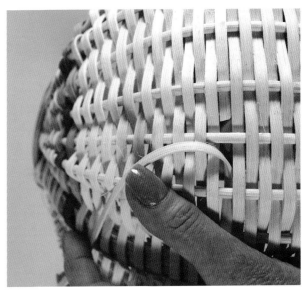

57 Tuck the weaver under several worked spokes.

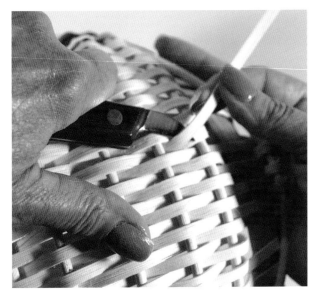

58 Cut the excess weaver.

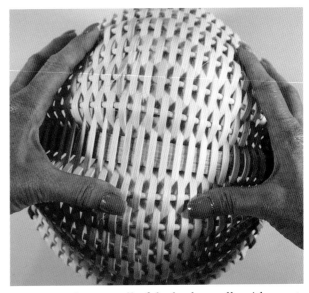

59 Redampen all of the basket walls with a wet sea sponge or large synthetic sponge. Use your fingers to gently redistribute the weavers into an even spacing until you are satisfied.

Wheel-Ear High Shoulder Melon Basket

Using a wheel ear creates space to add one or more spokes above the rim hoop in your basket. Adding more spokes above the rim hoop will narrow the basket opening near the handle, which may limit its utility in certain ways, but you can still use it for a lot of things, and the finished effect is quite charming. This basket mainly uses an O1U1 weaving pattern but also includes some seagrass twining with extra twists. It's a pretty simple project, so go ahead and tackle it even if you haven't had much practice yet. I call the dyed version the "peach basket."

SUPPLIES

- Two 6" diameter x ½" width (15.3 x 1.3cm) oak hoops
- 1 yard (1m) of twine
- Measuring tape
- Pencil
- Scissors or reed cutters
- Craft knife
- Flat packing tool
- Soaking pan and warm water
- 220-grit sandpaper
- Nylon-grip flat-nosed pliers
- Red powdered drink mix, water, bowl, and latex gloves
- Spray-on polyurethane sealer

SPOKES AND WEAVERS

- ¼" natural flat reed (wheel ear, Weave 1, 3, 5)
- 2.5mm cane (Weave 3)
- #4 round reed (Spoke Set 1)
- 3mm braided seagrass (Weave 2, 4)

SPOKE CUTTING

- Spoke Set 1: cut 6 total from #4 round reed
  All spokes 8½" (21.6cm)

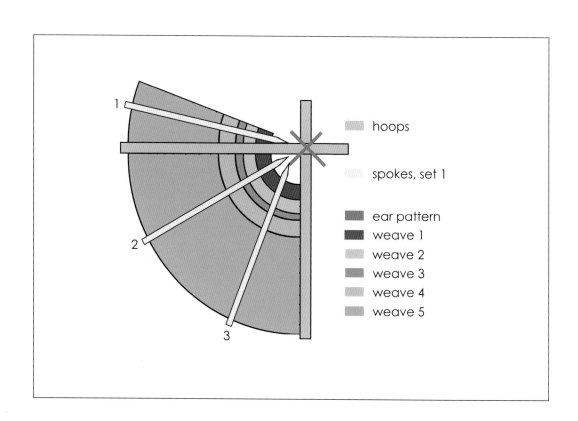

- hoops
- spokes, set 1
- ear pattern
- weave 1
- weave 2
- weave 3
- weave 4
- weave 5

Wheel Ear (¼" natural flat reed)

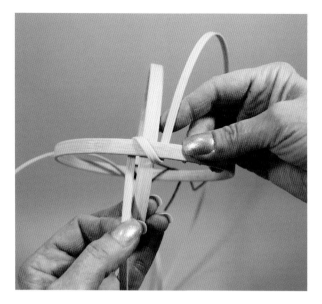

1 Make a pencil mark on one spot on one hoop. Use a measuring tape to determine the circumference of the hoop, divide that number by 2, and use this measurement to make a mark exactly halfway around the hoop, directly opposite the first mark you made. Repeat the entire marking process with the second hoop. Insert the handle hoop inside the rim hoop, matching up the pencil marks. Use twine to temporarily tie the two hoops together where they intersect on both sides. Start working a wheel ear with 6 rows using ¼" flat reed. (If you need extra guidance, see page 73.) Begin with the X cross in the center.

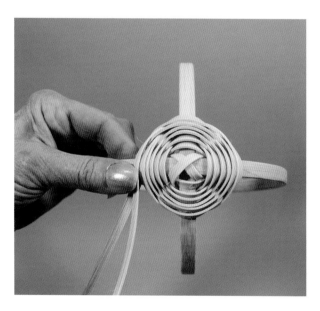

2 When you are done with the wheel ear, tuck and cut the excess reed.

Spoke Set 1

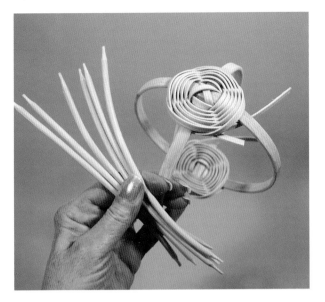

3 Soak a length of #4 round reed in your water pan. Place one end of the reed at the center of one wheel ear. Bend it along the rim hoop and mark where the reed meets the center of the other wheel ear. Cut the reed at this mark, which is about half of the circumference of the rim hoop. Cut five more spokes of the same size, for a total of six. Alternatively, cut the spokes following the measurements given in the Spoke Cutting list on page 150. Taper each end of each spoke to a point with a craft knife.

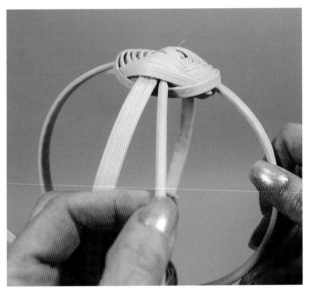

4 Insert all of the spokes. Spoke #1 is inserted into the loop of the wheel ear just above the rim hoop. Spoke #2 goes into the loop of the wheel ear just below the rim hoop. Spoke #3 goes into the loop of the wheel ear right next to the spine.

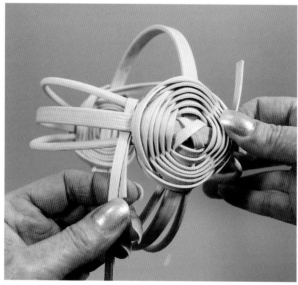
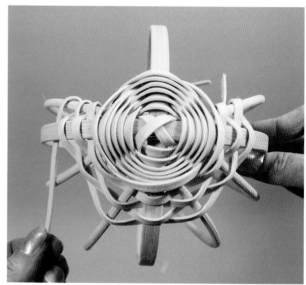

5 Using ¼" natural flat reed, work 5 rows of O1U1 weaving. Work the weaving, treating the topmost spoke like any regular spoke and the rim like just another spoke. Tuck and cut the excess reed.

Weave 2 (3mm braided seagrass)

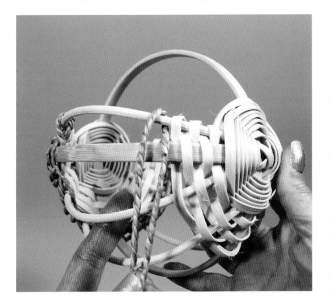
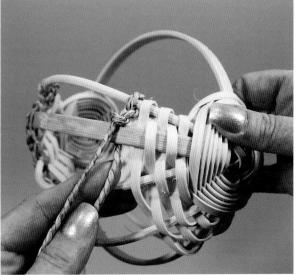
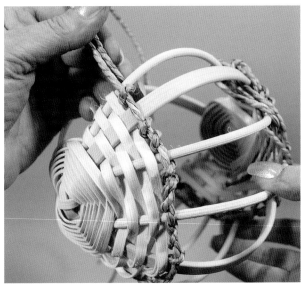
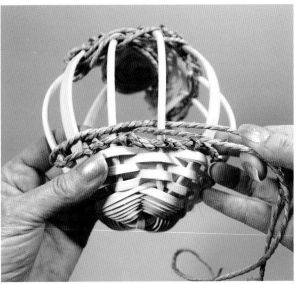

6 Using 3mm braided seagrass, work 2 rows of twining, adding one twist in each space between the spokes (see page 100) on the first row but not the second row. Tuck and cut.

Weave 3 (¼" natural flat reed and 2.5mm cane)

 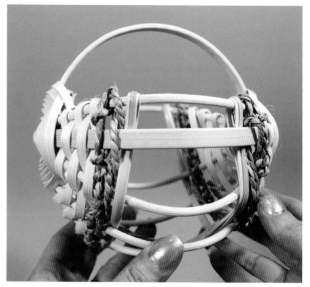

7 Measure a piece of ¼" natural flat reed long enough to create 1 row of weaving across the basket. Cut a piece of 2.5mm cane to the same length. Lay the cane over the flat reed and work the two together as one weaver, with the cane on top. Work 1 row of O1U1 weaving. Tuck and cut.

Weave 4 (3mm braided seagrass)

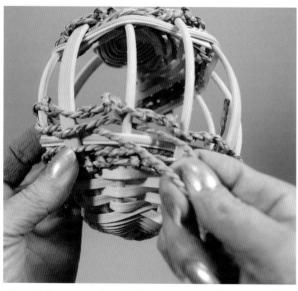 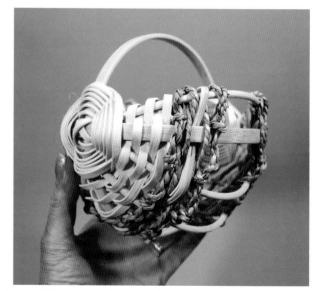

8 Using 3mm braided seagrass, work 2 rows of twining, adding one twist in each space between the spokes on the second row but not the first row. Tuck and cut.

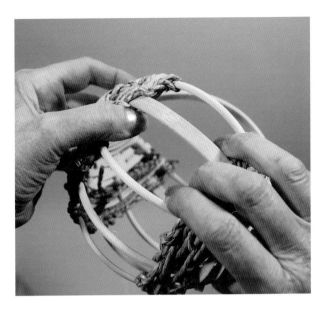

9 At this point, pack the rows. The two twining rows in particular should be packable or left looser in places so that you do not need any short rows to evenly fill the sides of this small basket.

Weave 5 (¼" natural flat reed)

Dyeing

10 Using ¼" natural flat reed, work 11 rows of O1U1 weaving (or as many as necessary) to fill in the rest of the basket.

11 Allow your basket to dry completely overnight. Check your packing and clip any long reeds left over. Follow the instructions described on page 32 to dye this basket a soft but eye-catching pink.

Wheel-Ear High Shoulder Melon Basket ■ **157**

CHAPTER 4

ADDITIONAL BASKETS

I n this chapter, you can pick and choose from twelve diverse, fun baskets that range from easy to challenging. Instead of the comprehensive step-by-step approach used in Chapter 3, these projects are presented with the essential information only: the materials needed, the spoke lengths, a diagram, and a basic explanation of steps. **If you are new to basketry, I strongly recommend that you work through at least one of the full-instruction basket designs in Chapter 3 before you begin the projects in this section.** If you haven't completed one of the baskets in Chapter 3, you can still try to tackle these baskets, but you might find yourself confused at points. Refer to the basket instructions in Chapter 3 and to the information in Chapters 1 and 2 if at any point you find yourself stuck or unsure about how to do a certain technique or achieve a certain effect.

All of the projects in this chapter will require the standard basket-making materials discussed earlier in the book and listed in the supplies lists for the step-by-step projects in Chapter 3. These may include (but are not limited to) twine, a measuring tape, a pencil, a soaking pan and warm water, a flat packing tool, a craft knife or scissors, 220-grit sandpaper, and nylon-grip flat-nosed pliers. These items are not listed in the supplies lists for the projects in this chapter. As such, the supplies lists are shorter and formatted a little bit differently than they have been up to this point in the book.

In general, you can finish each basket in the following way, unless the basket gives specific finishing instructions: Allow the basket to dry well overnight. Lightly dampen with a spray bottle filled with clean water. Pack the weavers, working from the ear to the center. Add one more weaver if necessary. Seal your basket with your favorite sealer.

Note: All basket size measurements were made across the rim of the basket and from the rim of the basket to the floor. These measurements do not include added width where the basket belly flares out from the rim size.

Apple

This basket has a simple structure, but a charming wrapped handle and contrasting color choices make it pop.

God's Eye ear, oval melon
Basket dimensions, not including the handle: 9" (22.9cm) long x 8¼" (21cm) wide x 4¼" (10.8cm) deep, with the rim being the widest point of the basket

---

SUPPLIES AND WEAVERS

- Two 9" x ½" (22.9 x 1.3cm) hoops
- ¼" oak-dyed flat reed (handle wrapping, ear)
- ¼" natural flat reed (Weave 1)
- ½" half-round reed (spokes)
- ⅜" brown-dyed flat raffia ribbon (handle and rim wrapping)

SPOKES

Use ½" half-round reed. Cut 2 of each:
- #1: 12½" (31.8cm)
- #2: 12½" (31.8cm)

1 Wrap the handle hoop using ⅜" brown-dyed raffia ribbon and ¼" oak-dyed flat reed. Wrap the rim hoop with ⅜" brown-dyed raffia ribbon.

2 Measure the circumference of each hoop and mark the halfway point on both sides of both hoops with a pencil. Insert the handle hoop inside the rim hoop, matching the marks. Tie temporarily with twine.

3 Using ¼" oak-dyed flat reed, work a God's Eye ear for 5 rows (ear pattern).

4 Insert the two spokes into the God's Eye ear.

5 Using ¼" natural flat reed, work the basket sides in an O1U1 pattern (Weave 1). Work all the way to the center of the basket. At the center, pack the reed as necessary to maintain the weaving pattern with the final, center row.

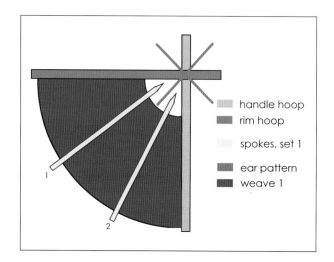

handle hoop
rim hoop
spokes, set 1
ear pattern
weave 1

Cantaloupe

This basket works with extra-thin spokes and rolls every other weaver over the top spoke instead of the rim. A single section of dried leaves adds contrast.

Half God's Eye ear, flat bottom melon
Basket dimensions, not including the handle: 10¼" (26cm) long x 10" (25.4cm) wide x 6" (15.2cm) deep, with the rim being the widest point of the basket

SUPPLIES AND WEAVERS
- Two 10" x ¾" (25.4 x 2cm) hoops
- ¼" flat reed (ear, Weave 4)
- ⅜" flat reed (Weave 6)
- #2 round reed (spokes)
- #1 round reed (Weave 1, 3, 5)
- Dried lily, iris, or pampas grass leaves (Weave 2)

SPOKES
Use #2 round reed. Cut 2 of each:

Spoke Set 1
- #1: 14" (35.6cm)
- #2: 14" (35.6cm)
- #3: 14" (35.6cm)
- #4: 16" (40.6cm)
- #5: 16½" (41.9cm)
- #6: 16½" (41.9cm)

Spoke Set 2
- #7: 14½" (36.8cm)
- #8: 15½" (39.4cm)
- #9: 16½" (41.9cm)

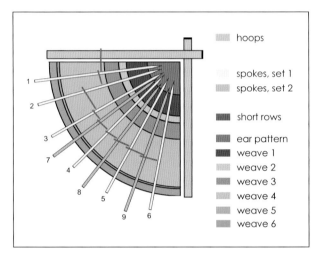

hoops

spokes, set 1
spokes, set 2

short rows

ear pattern
weave 1
weave 2
weave 3
weave 4
weave 5
weave 6

1 Measure the circumference of each hoop and mark the halfway point on both sides of both hoops with a pencil. Insert the handle hoop inside the rim hoop, matching the marks. Tie temporarily with twine.

2 Using ¼" flat reed, work a half God's Eye for 9 rows (ear pattern).

3 Insert spokes #1 through #6, following the chart for placement. These spokes are unusually thin round reeds and will bend easily as you work.

4 Using #1 round reed, work 11 rows of O1U1 weaving (Weave 1).

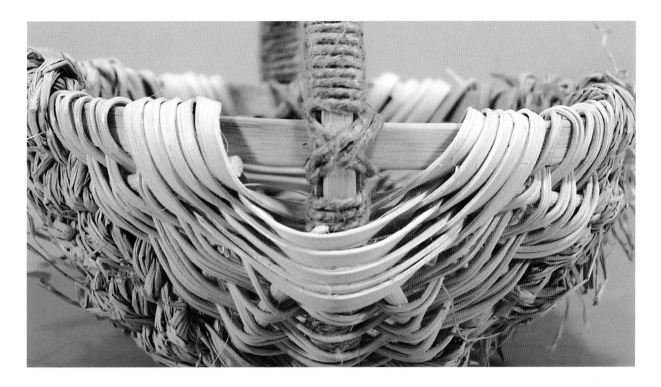

3 Cut two lengths of burlap cord 2 yards (2m) each. Measure and mark 2" (5cm) above the hoop intersection on the top portion of the handle. Lay 2" (5cm) of your cord onto the center of the handle hoop with the end of the cord pointed down. At the mark, begin wrapping the cord around the handle hoop and the cord end, working toward the hoop intersection.

4 At the hoop intersection, create a double X knot ear with the cord (ear pattern). Continue wrapping the cord around the handle hoop for 2" (5cm) below the intersection. Loosen several wraps, tuck the end of the cord under these loops, and pull tightly. Trim any excess cord.

5 Using ¼" flat reed, work 5 rows of a half God's Eye (Weave 1).

6 Insert spokes #1 and #3 into the side loops of the half God's Eye. Make a hole in the crossover of the half God's Eye with an awl for spoke #2.

7 Using two strands of #2 round reed worked together as one weaver, work 10 rows of arrow twining to create a double arrow twine pattern (Weave 2).

8 Insert spokes #4 and #5 into the arrow twining.

9 Using twisted raffia cord, fill the remaining section of the basket side with arrow twining (Weave 3). My basket required 26 rows, which created thirteen arrows.

Grape

This is a stunning, unique basket due to its use of grapevine and the inclusion of side openings, giving you more than one way to pick up the basket.

Braided God's Eye ear with half God's Eye, melon
Basket dimensions, not including the handle: 6½" (16.5cm) long x 5½" (14cm) wide x 3¼" (8.3cm) deep x 6¾" (17.1cm) at the widest point of the basket sides

SUPPLIES AND WEAVERS

- Two 5" x ½" (12.7 x 1.3cm) round hoops
- ¼" walnut-dyed flat reed (handle wrapping)
- ¼" flat reed (Weave 4)
- 2.5mm cane (handle wrapping, ear, Weave 1, 2, 3)
- #4 round reed (spokes)
- #2 round reed (rim accent)
- Dried grapevine (rim accent)

SPOKES

Use #4 round reed. Cut 2 of each:
- #1: 8½" (21.6cm)
- #2: 8½" (21.6cm)
- #3: 9½" (24.1cm)

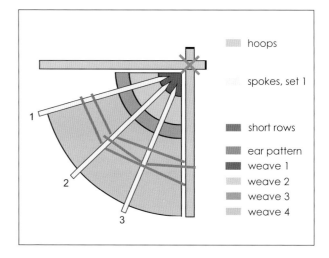

▨	hoops
	spokes, set 1
▨	short rows
▨	ear pattern
▨	weave 1
▨	weave 2
▨	weave 3
▨	weave 4

1 Measure the circumference of each hoop and mark the halfway point on both sides of both hoops with a pencil. Insert the handle hoop inside the rim hoop, matching the marks. Tie temporarily with twine.

2 Wrap the handle using ¼" walnut-dyed flat reed and 2.5mm cane.

3 Using 2.5mm cane, work a 4-row braided God's Eye (ear pattern).

4 Continuing with the 2.5mm cane, create a 7-row half God's Eye (Weave 1).

5 Insert spokes #1 and #3 into the side loops of the half God's Eye. Make a hole in the crossover of the half God's Eye with an awl for spoke #2.

6 Using 2.5mm cane, work the O1U1 pattern for 3 rows (Weave 2).

ADDITIONAL BASKETS

1 Measure the circumference of the hoop and mark the halfway point on both sides of the hoop with a pencil.

2 Measure 1" (2.5cm) down from each end of the #8 round reed spine. Hold it inside the rim hoop like a handle hoop, matching the marks, with the 1" (2.5cm) extending above the rim hoop. Mark the width of the hoop on the round reed on both ends. With a craft knife, cut away a section from the round reed so that it fits flatly against the hoop on both ends. Secure both ends of the reed against the rim hoop with a spring clamp.

3 Using 3mm cane, work a half God's Eye ear for 8 rows (ear pattern).

4 Insert spokes #1 through #5, following the chart.

5 Using natural-colored raffia strands, work 3 rows of O1U1 weaving. Tie the ends of this raffia into square knots on the outside of the basket for added decoration (Weave 1).

6 Add spokes #6, #7, and #8, following the chart.

7 With #1 or #2 round reed, weave 5 rows of arrow twining to create two and a half arrows (Weave 2).

8 Insert spoke #9. This spoke lies just ¼" (0.6cm) to ⅜" (1cm) below the rim hoop.

9 Using natural-colored raffia strands, work 6 rows of arrow twining (Weave 3). Tie the ends of this raffia into square knots on the outside of the basket for added decoration.

10 Using ¼" turquoise-dyed flat reed, work 5 rows of O1U1 weaving (Weave 4). Start rows 1, 3, and 5 of this section of weaving on the top spoke rather than the rim to create short rows.

11 Using #1 or #2 round reed worked with three strands at a time, create 2 rows of arrow twining (making one full arrow) (Weave 5).

12 With twisted raffia cord, work 1 row of twisted twining (Weave 6). Begin this row on spoke #9. Tie the ends of the raffia cord on the outside of the basket to add an area of decoration.

13 A lemon-wedge short row area is worked next to compensate for the changing diameter of the basket (Weave 7). This area is worked using ¼" oak-dyed flat reed. Begin the wedge on spoke #4, the second spoke from the spine. With each new row, roll the reed over two spokes above the roll of the previous row. Continue in this manner until you have worked 8 rows.

14 Roll row 9 and 10 of the lemon wedge on the same spoke as row 8. Roll rows 11, 12, and 13 on spoke #1.

15 Using ¼" turquoise-dyed flat reed, work 1 row of O1U1 weaving, beginning on spoke #9. Work another row, this time turning on the rim hoop. Work a third row, turning on spoke #9 (Weave 8).

16 The center weaver is done using ¾" flat reed and worked as an individual row (Weave 9).

Oregano

Large acrylic beads accent the curve of the round reed arrow twining in this basket. Three vertical central spokes added to each side of the spine stretch the shape of the basket out lengthwise.

Double bow ear with three-spoke lashing with X pattern, low oval egg
Basket dimensions, not including the handle: 9" (22.9cm) long x 8¼" (21cm) wide x 4¼" (10.8cm) deep x 10½" (26.7cm) at the widest point of the basket sides

SUPPLIES AND WEAVERS
- Two 8" x ½" (20.3 x 1.3cm) hoops
- 16 large-hole acrylic beads
- Acrylic glue
- ⅜" flat reed (ear)
- ¼" flat reed (Weave 1, 2, 5, 6)
- #4 round reed (spokes)
- #2 round reed (Weave 3)
- 3mm jute cord (Weave 4)

SPOKES
Use #4 round reed. Cut 2 of each:

Spoke Set 1
- #1: 16¼" (41.3cm)
- #2: 17" (43.2cm)
- #3: 17" (43.2cm)

Spoke Set 2
- #4: 8½" (21.6cm)
- #5: 14¼" (36.2cm)
- #6: 7" (17.8cm)

Spoke Set 3
- #7: 6" (15.2cm)
- #8: 8" (20.3cm)

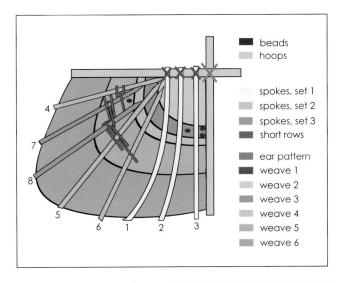

▉	beads
▉	hoops
▉	spokes, set 1
▉	spokes, set 2
▉	spokes, set 3
▉	short rows
▉	ear pattern
▉	weave 1
▉	weave 2
▉	weave 3
▉	weave 4
▉	weave 5
▉	weave 6

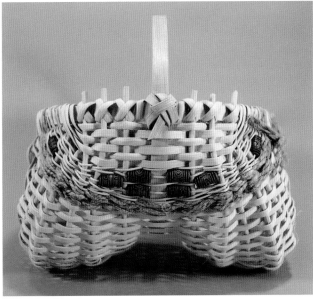

1 Measure the circumference of each hoop and mark the halfway point on both sides of both hoops with a pencil. Insert the handle hoop inside the rim hoop, matching the marks. Tie temporarily with twine.

2 Using ⅜" flat reed, create a double bow knot ear at the intersection of the hoops (ear pattern).

3 Cut spokes #1 through #3 from #4 round reed. With a craft knife, notch the top ¾" (2cm) of the back side of both ends of the spokes. Measure and mark ¾" (2cm) from the handle hoop for the placement of spoke #3. Mark ¾" (2cm) away from spoke #3 for the placement of spoke #2. Measure again at ¾" (2cm) away from spoke #2 for the placement of spoke #1. Place the spokes onto their marks and clamp into place with a small spring clamp.

4 Using ¼" flat reed, work a three-spoke lashing with X pattern ear (Weave 1). Do not cut the reed.

5 Continuing with the ¼" flat reed, begin weaving in an O1U1 pattern, working 6 rows (Weave 2).

6 Insert spokes #4, #5, and #6. Spokes #4 and #5 go behind the top loop, just below the rim, of the weaving from step 3. Spoke #6 goes in the same loop that covers spoke #1, lying on the outside of this spoke.

7 Using #2 round reed, work 12 rows of arrow twining, creating six arrows (Weave 3). On the second row, add one large bead in the space between spoke #3 and the handle on both sides of the handle. Do this by sliding both working strands of round reed through the hole in the bead. On the fifth row, add one large bead in the space between spoke #2 and spoke #3 on both sides. On the seventh row, add one large bead in the space between spoke #3 and the handle on both sides. Add the last bead on the ninth row in the space between spoke #4 and #5 on both sides.

8 Using two extra-long strands of jute cord together as one weaver, work 3 rows of arrow twining (Weave 4). To do this, fold the cords in half lengthwise and lay them over the rim. This places two cords in front of the rim and two behind. End this weaving by tying a square knot with the four strands just under the rim. Cut the excess strands to about 2" (5cm) long.

9 Insert spokes #7 and #8 into the jute weaving.

10 Using ¼" flat reed, work 4 rows of O1U1 weaving (Weave 5).

11 Now it's time to make some short rows with ¼" flat reed (continuing Weave 5). Begin the first short row on spoke #4. Work the row to the opposite side of the basket on spoke #4. Repeat until you have two short row turns on spoke #4. Next, turn your weaver at spoke #7 and work until you have created two turns over spoke #7. Next, turn your weaver at spoke #8 and work until you have created two turns over spoke #8.

12 Using ¼" flat reed, work 11 full rows in an O1U1 pattern or until you have filled the side of the basket (Weave 6).

13 Because the pattern from Weave 5 is at a dramatic angle to the weaving down the side of the basket from Weave 6, you will want to allow this basket to dry overnight before you pack your weavers. Pack the inner weavers first, working them toward the hoop handle. Then pack the side weavers into the short row turns. Add one or two extra ¼" flat reed weavers if necessary.

Raspberry

This basket mixes extra-thin and extra-wide weavers to create interesting contrast, with pops of bright red to boot.

Double X ear, melon
Basket dimensions, not including the handle: 8¾" (22.2cm) long x 8½" (21.6cm) wide x 4" (10.2cm) deep, with the rim being the widest point of the basket

SUPPLIES AND WEAVERS
- Two 8" x ½" (20.3 x 1.3cm) hoops
- ½" (1.3cm) maple splint (ear)
- ¼" walnut-dyed flat reed (handle wrapping)
- ½" oval flat reed (spokes)
- ¼" natural flat reed (Weave 2, 4)
- ¼" oak-dyed flat reed (Weave 5)
- 2mm cane (Weave 1)
- Natural raffia strands (handle wrapping)
- Red-dyed raffia strands (handle wrapping, Weave 3)

SPOKES
Use ½" oval flat reed. Cut 2 of each:

Spoke Set 1
- #1: 9" (22.9cm)

Spoke Set 2
- #2: 9½" (24.1cm)
- #3: 9½" (24.1cm)

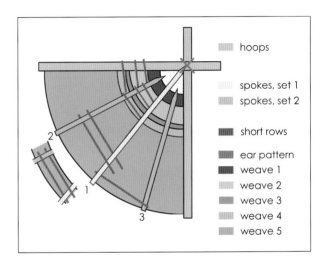

hoops

spokes, set 1
spokes, set 2

short rows

ear pattern
weave 1
weave 2
weave 3
weave 4
weave 5

1 Using natural raffia, red-dyed raffia, and ¼" walnut-dyed flat reed, create a decorative handle hoop wrap on one half of the hoop.

2 Measure the circumference of each hoop and mark the halfway point on both sides of both hoops with a pencil. Insert the handle hoop inside the rim hoop, matching the marks. Tie temporarily with twine.

3 With ½" (1.3cm) maple splint, work a double X ear to join the two hoops (ear pattern).

4 Insert spoke #1 under the rim hoop and into the back loop of ear.

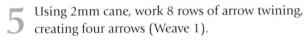

5 Using 2mm cane, work 8 rows of arrow twining, creating four arrows (Weave 1).

6 Add spoke #2 into the weave above spoke #1. Add spoke #3 into the weave below spoke #1.

7 Using ¼" natural flat reed, work 4 rows of O1U1 weaving (Weave 2). Create short rows by turning the second and fourth of these 4 rows on spoke #2 (the top spoke).

8 Using red-dyed raffia, work 4 rows of twining (Weave 3).

9 Using ¼" natural flat reed, work 2 rows of O1U1 weaving, turning the second row on spoke #2 (the top spoke) (Weave 4).

10 Using ¼" oak-dyed flat reed, work 7 rows of O1U1 weaving (Weave 5).

11 Using ¼" oak-dyed flat reed, fill the remaining area of the basket wall with 5 short rows (still Weave 5). Begin these rows on spoke #2 (the top spoke) for two rows, and on spoke #1 (the second spoke) for the central, third row. The last two short rows fall on the opposite side of the central row.

Rosemary

The wrapped weaving pattern in this basket, worked in an arrow design, allows for a large amount of space between each row, creating an interesting, airy feel.

Three-point lashing ear, full melon
Basket dimensions, not including the handle: 7½" (19cm) long x 5½" (14cm) wide x 4½" (11.4cm) deep, with the rim being the widest point of the basket

SUPPLIES AND WEAVERS

- Two 6" x ½" (15.2 x 1.3cm) hoops
- ¼" flat reed (Weave 2)
- 3mm cane (ear, Weave 1)
- #3 to #5 round reed (spokes)
- #1 or #2 round reed (Weave 3)

SPOKES

Use #3 to #5 round reed. Cut 2 of each:

- #1: 9" (22.9cm)
- #2: 9½" (24.1cm)
- #3: 9½" (24.1cm)

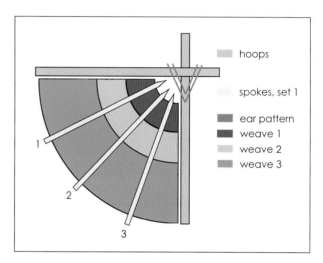

1   Measure the circumference of each hoop and mark the halfway point on both sides of both hoops with a pencil. Insert the handle hoop inside the rim hoop, matching the marks. Tie temporarily with twine.

2   Using 3mm cane, work a three-point lashing ear for 6 rows (ear pattern).

3   Add all of the spokes, evenly spacing them across the wall area. Secure the ends of the spokes under the sides of the ear.

4   Continuing with the 3mm cane, work 6 rows of O1U1 weaving (Weave 1).

5   Using ¼" flat reed, work 4 individual rows (Weave 2). Start the first and third rows by rolling over spoke #1. Work the second and fourth rows over the rim hoop.

6 Using #1 or #2 round reed, work a wrapped weave in the arrow pattern to completely fill the remaining space (Weave 3). Begin the wrap weave by securing your #1 or #2 round reed under the ¼" flat reed at the center bottom hoop. Bring the weaver outside the frame between the center bottom hoop and spoke #3. Roll the weaver over spoke #3 to create one wrap. Move the weaver over the top of spoke #2 and roll the weaver over the spoke. Repeat two more times for spoke #1 and for the rim hoop. This creates one half row. Continue the wrapping pattern, working full rows from rim hoop to rim hoop, until the center of the basket is filled. Work one half row to bring the round reed to the center bottom hoop. Secure the end of the weaver under the adjacent ¼" flat reed. Cut the excess round reed.

Spearmint

This basket features a ragged robin design using the leftover reeds from the other projects made for this book and also uses as many weaving patterns as possible.

Three-spoke lashing with bar pattern ear, low oval
Basket dimensions: 6" (15.2cm) long x 6½" (16.5cm) wide x 4¾" (12cm) deep x 8" (20.3cm) at the widest point of the basket sides

SUPPLIES AND WEAVERS
- One 6" x ½" (15.2 x 1.3cm) hoop
- 3mm cane (ear)
- #5 to #8 round reed (spine, spokes)
- Assorted scrap weavers, including:
  - #2 round reed, dyed several colors
  - Twisted raffia cord or colored paper cord
  - Loose raffia strands
  - Burlap string
  - 3mm twisted seagrass
  - ½" flat reed

SPOKES
For the spine, use #5 to #8 round reed. Cut 6 total, 14" (35.6cm) long.
For the rest of the spokes, use #5 to #8 round reed. Cut 2 of each:

Spoke Set 1
- #1: 10" (25.4cm)
- #2: 11" (27.9cm)
- #3: 10" (25.4cm)

Spoke Set 2
- #4: 7" (17.8cm)
- #5: 7" (17.8cm)
- #6: 8½" (21.6cm)

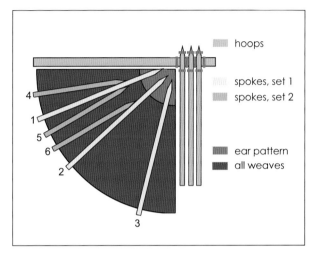

1 Measure the circumference of the hoop and mark the halfway point on both sides of the hoop with a pencil. Measure ½" (1.3cm) from the center points on both sides of the points and mark with a pencil.

2 Measure and cut the three spokes that will serve as the spine from #5 to #8 round reed. Measure ¼" (0.6cm) down from each end of each length of round reed and mark with a pencil. Measure ½" (1.3cm) down from this pencil mark and make a second mark. Using a craft knife, cut out a slice of reed between these two marks to create a flat area that will rest against the rim hoop.

3 Position these reeds on the outside of the rim hoop at the pencil marks. Use a spring clamp to hold them in place.

4 Using 3mm cane, work a three-spoke lashing with bar ear to secure the reeds (ear pattern).

5 Continuing with the 3mm cane, work a half God's Eye ear, working over all three spine spokes (still ear pattern). Work this pattern for 8 rows. Because you are working the half God's Eye over multiple spokes, this ear pattern becomes a long half-oval shape.

6 Using your leftover weavers, work each row of this basket design as individual rows (except for the arrow twining sections), tucking the reed under at each side and clipping the excess reed. Use a variety of weaving patterns and mix your textured or colored weavers randomly with your natural colored reed. Insert the spokes following the chart when it seems logical to do so. The weaving pattern used for this exact basket is as follows:

- 1 row of #1 dark brown round reed in twining pattern
- 2 rows of #1 natural round reed in arrow twining
- 2 rows of #1 dark brown round reed in arrow twining
- 2 rows of dark green paper cord in arrow twining
- 1 row of ¼" flat reed worked in O1U1
- 1 row of twisted raffia cord worked in O1U1
- 1 row of ¼" flat reed worked in O1U1
- 1 row of 3mm cane worked in O1U1
- 1 row of dark green paper cord worked in wrapped weaving with the bar inside
- 1 row of twisted raffia cord worked in wrapped weaving with the bar inside
- 1 short row of ¼" flat reed worked in O1U1, starting and ending on the fifth spoke from the rim hoop
- 1 short row of ¼" flat reed worked in O1U1, starting and ending on the fourth spoke from the rim hoop
- 1 short row of ¼" flat reed worked in O1U1, starting and ending on the first spoke from the rim hoop
- 1 short row of ¼" flat reed worked in O1U1, starting and ending on the second spoke from the rim hoop
- 1 short row of ¼" flat reed worked in O1U1, starting and ending on the first spoke from the rim hoop
- 1 short row of ½" flat reed worked in O1U1, starting and ending on the first spoke from the rim hoop
- 1 row of 3mm twisted seagrass worked in wrapped weaving with the bar inside
- 1 row (center row to finish the basket walls) of ½" flat reed worked in O1U1

Spring Onion

This stunning basket includes two sizes of spokes as well as a very wide cut and tapered flat reed for a short row.

Two-point lashing with collar ear, low oval

Basket dimensions, not including the handle: 6" (15.2cm) long x 5¾" (14.6cm) wide x 3¼" (8.3cm) deep x 7¼" (18.4cm) at the widest point of the basket sides

SUPPLIES AND WEAVERS

- Two 6" x ½" (15.2 x 1.3cm) hoops
- ¼" oval flat reed (ear, Weave 3)
- ½" oval flat reed (Spoke Set 1)
- ¾" flat reed (Weave 2)
- 2.5mm cane (Weave 1, 4)
- #3 or #4 round reed (Spoke Set 2)

SPOKES

Use ½" oval flat reed for spokes #1–#3. Use #3 or #4 round reed for spokes #4–#5. Cut 2 of each:

Spoke Set 1
- #1: 11" (27.9cm)
- #2: 11" (27.9cm)
- #3: 10" (25.4cm)

Spoke Set 2
- #4: 7" (17.8cm)
- #5: 6" (15.2cm)

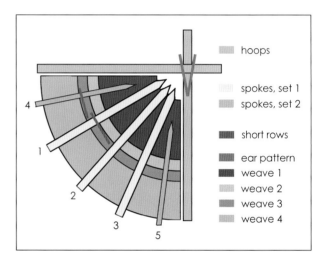

hoops

spokes, set 1
spokes, set 2

short rows
ear pattern
weave 1
weave 2
weave 3
weave 4

1 Measure the circumference of each hoop and mark the halfway point on both sides of both hoops with a pencil. Insert the handle hoop inside the rim hoop, matching the marks. Tie temporarily with twine.

2 Using ¼" oval flat reed, work a two-point lashing with collar ear for 7 rows (ear pattern).

3 Insert spokes #1, #2, and #3. The ends of these spokes rest between the handle hoop and the side walls of the ear.

4 Using 2.5mm cane, work 10 rows of O1U1 weaving (Weave 1).

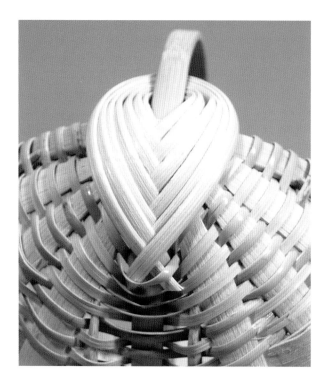

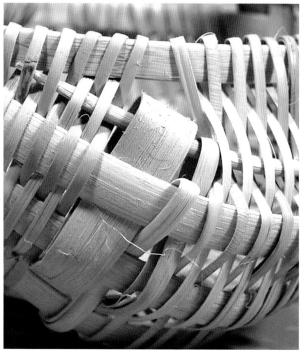

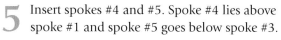

5 Insert spokes #4 and #5. Spoke #4 lies above spoke #1 and spoke #5 goes below spoke #3.

6 Using 2.5mm cane, work 4–5 more rows of O1U1 weaving (still Weave 1). The last row of this weaving set should have the weaver on top of the spine.

7 Measure a length of ¾" flat reed to the circumference of the basket where the next row of weaving will fall. Add 6" (15.2cm) to your measurement: 3" (7.6cm) per side. Measure and mark the center point of this length of reed. Measure and mark 3" (7.6cm) on both sides of the center mark.

8 With a craft knife, cut and taper this central 6" (15.2cm) area of the ¾" flat reed to ¼" (0.6cm) wide at the center point. This creates a weaver that begins at ¾" (2cm) wide, tapers to ¼" (0.6cm) at the center, and then returns to ¾" (2cm) wide.

9 Feed this altered weaver under the spine and weave from this point to the rim hoop on both sides in an O1U1 pattern (Weave 2).

10 Using ¼" oval flat reed, work 1 individual short row, starting the row on spoke #1 (the second spoke). Then work 1 more individual short row, starting the row on spoke #4 (the top spoke) (Weave 3).

11 Using 2.5mm cane, fill the remaining open space of the basket wall with O1U1 weaving (Weave 4).

Thyme

This special basket includes beads added to the weavers and above-the-rim spokes that slightly reduce the size of the basket opening.

Two-point lashing with collar ear, low egg
Basket dimensions, not including the handle: 6½" (16.5cm) long x 5" (12.7cm) wide x 4¼" (10.8cm) deep x 6¼" (15.9cm) at the widest point of the basket sides

SUPPLIES AND WEAVERS

- Two 6" x ½" (15.2 x 1.3cm) hoops
- 24 plastic 8mm large-hole beads
- ¼" flat reed (ear)
- #3 to #5 round reed (spokes)
- #1 or #2 round reed (Weave 1, 2, 4)
- 3 colors of raffia string (Weave 3)

SPOKES

Use #3 to #5 round reed. Cut 2 of each:

Spoke Set 1
- #1: 12" (30.5cm)

Spoke Set 2
- #2: 9" (22.9cm)
- #3: 10" (25.4cm)
- #4: 11" (27.9cm)

Spoke Set 3
- #5: 9" (22.9cm)

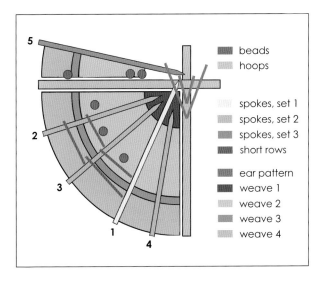

1 Measure the circumference of each hoop and mark the halfway point on both sides of both hoops with a pencil. Insert the handle hoop inside the rim hoop, matching the marks. Tie temporarily with twine.

2 Using ¼" flat reed, create a two-point lashing with collar ear, working the ear for 4 rows (ear pattern).

3 Insert spoke #1 between the ear and the rim hoop. Position it below the center diagonal line of the side wall area.

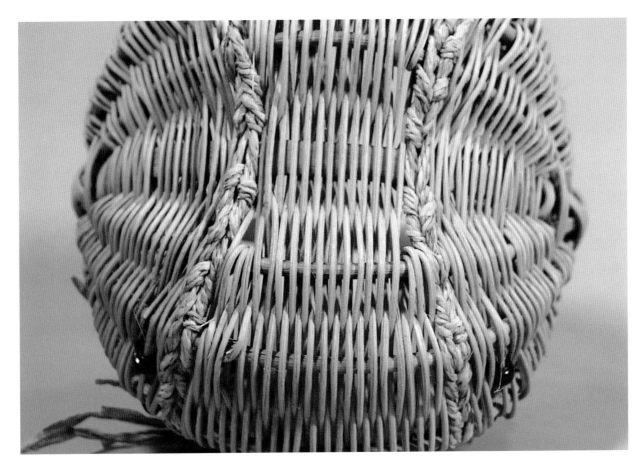

4 Using #1 or #2 round reed, work 3 rows of arrow twining to create one and a half arrows (Weave 1).

5 Insert spokes #2, #3, and #4 into the arrow twining. Spokes #2 and #3 go above spoke #1, and spoke #4 goes below spoke #1.

6 Using #1 or #2 round reed, work 8 rows of arrow twining, continuing the pattern established in step 4 (Weave 2).

7 Insert spoke #5 above the rim hoop, securing it under the upper side of the ear.

8 Bring your round reed arrow twining over the spoke above the rim hoop (still Weave 2). Add one bead to the reed. Roll the weaver over the spoke, then thread it back through the bead. The bead now lies between the top spoke and the rim hoop and captures the reed twice. Work the round reed for 3 arrow twining rows.

9 Bring your round reed arrow twining over the spoke above the rim hoop (still Weave 2). Add one bead to the reed. Roll the weaver over the spoke, then thread it back through the bead. The bead now lies between the top spoke and the rim hoop and captures the reed twice. This adds a second bead (still Weave 2).

10 Work 4 arrow twining rows (still Weave 2).

11 Create a short row area by rolling the round reed over spoke #2 twice, then rolling the reed over spoke #3 twice, and finally rolling the reed over spoke #1 once (still Weave 2).

12 Return the round reed weaver to the spoke above the rim (spoke #5). Roll over the top spoke and rim in the arrow twining pattern. Add one bead to the reed in the space between the rim and spoke #2.

13 Work the next row in the arrow twining pattern over the next spoke, adding a bead to the reed in the space below this spoke, spoke #3 (still Weave 2).

14 Repeat step 12 one more time for a total of three added beads in a row (still Weave 2).

15 Work the round reed for 1 more arrow twining row (still Weave 2).

16 Using three strands of colored raffia as one weaver, work 2 rows of twisted twining (Weave 3). Tie the ends of the raffia strands on the outside of the basket to add a touch of decoration.

17 The remaining open wall space is worked using #1 or #2 round reed in the twining pattern (Weave 4). Begin a second area of short row work by rolling the first 2 rows over the first spoke below the rim hoop. Work the next 2 rows by turning or rolling the weaver over the rim hoop.

18 Work 1 row of twining, rolling over spoke #5. Add one bead to the reed in the space between the above-the-rim spoke #5 and the rim hoop.

19 Continue working the round reed in the twining pattern to the center of the basket.

Winter Melon

Round reed used for the ear and an exaggerated spoke near the rim both contribute to the unique look of this basket.

God's Eye ear with half God's Eye, flat bottom melon
Basket dimensions, not including the handle: 9" (22.9cm) long x 7¾" (19.7cm) wide x 4" (10.2cm) deep x 9½" (24.1cm) at the widest point of the basket sides

SUPPLIES AND WEAVERS

- Two 8" x ½" (20.3 x 1.3cm) hoops
- ¼" space-dyed flat reed (Weave 2, 6, 7)
- #2 round reed (ear, Weave 1)
- #4 round reed (spokes)
- Dried sedge grass or loose raffia (Weave 3)
- 4mm jute cord (Weave 4)
- Paper twist cords in medium brown, dark brown, and light yellow (Weave 5)

SPOKES

Use #4 round reed. Cut 2 of each:

Spoke Set 1
- #1: 13" (33cm)
- #2: 13" (33cm)
- #3: 13" (33cm)
- #4: 13" (33cm)

Spoke Set 2
- #5: 10" (25.4cm)
- #6: 10½" (26.7cm)
- #7: 11" (27.9cm)
- #8: 10" (25.4cm)

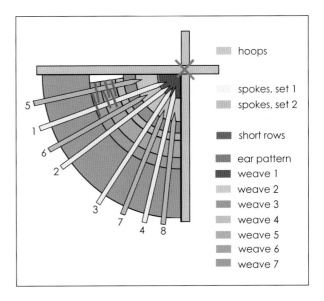

hoops

spokes, set 1

spokes, set 2

short rows

ear pattern

weave 1

weave 2

weave 3

weave 4

weave 5

weave 6

weave 7

1 Measure the circumference of each hoop and mark the halfway point on both sides of both hoops with a pencil. Insert the handle hoop inside the rim hoop, matching the marks. Tie temporarily with twine.

2 Using two lengths of #2 round reed together as one weaver, work a God's Eye ear for 3 rows (ear pattern).

3 Using two lengths of #2 round reed together as one weaver, work a half God's Eye ear for 5 rows (Weave 1).

4 Insert spokes #1 through #4 into the half God's Eye ear.

5 Using ¼" space-dyed flat reed, work 5 rows of O1U1 (Weave 2).

6 Insert spokes #5 through #8 into the previous weaving.

7 Using either dried sedge grass or loose raffia, work 2 rows of arrow twining (Weave 3).

8 Using 4mm jute cord, work 4 rows of arrow twining, beginning and ending on spoke #5 (Weave 4).

9 Using a double strand of paper twist cord, work 2 short rows of O1U1, beginning and ending on spoke #5 (Weave 5).

10 Work 1 individual short row of O1U1 with ¼" space-dyed flat reed, beginning and ending on spoke #5 (Weave 6).

11 Fill the remaining space on the basket side with ¼" space-dyed flat reed worked in O1U1 (Weave 7).

About the Author

Internationally known artist Lora S. Irish is the author of twenty-eight woodcarving, pyrography, and craft pattern books, including *Great Book of Carving Patterns*, *World Wildlife Patterns for the Scroll Saw*, *The Art and Craft of Pyrography*, *Relief Carving the Wood Spirit*, *Great Book of Celtic Patterns*, and many more. Winner of the Woodcarver of the Year award, Lora is a frequent contributor to *Woodcarving Illustrated* and *Scroll Saw Woodworking & Crafts* magazines. Working from her rural mid-Maryland home studio, she is currently exploring new crafts and hobbies, including wire bent-link jewelry, metal sheet jewelry, piece patch and appliqué quilting, gourd carving, gourd pyrography, and leather crafts.

Index